Empowered To Rise:

The Secret to Embracing Your True Identity, Uncovering Your Super Powers, and Bringing Your Inspiration to the World

David Trotter

Empowered to Rise: The Secret to Embracing Your True Identity, Uncovering Your Super Powers, and Bringing Your Inspiration to the World
by David Trotter

Designed by 8TRACKstudios - www.8trackstudios.com

ISBN: 978-1-935798-15-6

To Laura.
You are the strongest woman I know,
and I deeply admire your commitment
to empowering children to rise up.
Thank you for your grace,
love, and hard work.
You are loved.

INSPIRATION
Rising

SUBSCRIBE TO THE PODCAST
www.InspoRising.com/Podcast

JOIN OUR PRIVATE FACEBOOK
COMMUNITY FOR SUPPORT
www.InspoRising.com/Insiders

FOLLOW US ON SOCIAL MEDIA
@InspoRising

LAUNCH YOUR LIFE COACHING
www.InspoRising.com/Launch

TABLE OF CONTENTS

INTRODUCTION

Eight influential women molded and shaped me during the earliest years of my life...my mom plus seven elementary school teachers.

My mom did all the motherly things for me...loved, fed, bathed, clothed, and prepared me for school...not to mention giving birth to my almost-twelve-pound body three weeks after my due date.

Starting at age five, I spent hours each day with *women* who were committed to my success. Mrs. Hewitt taught me how to read and write - two skills I have gone on to use every single day of my life (even though I still hold the pencil wrong. So sorry!) How many skills have you learned from a single individual that have transformed your life like reading and writing?

These teachers taught me how to add, subtract, multiply, and divide, how to work well with others, how to play kickball and dodge ball, and most importantly...how to avoid dysentery on the Oregon Trail!

As a freshman in high school, I took a journalism class taught by a *woman* who gave me the opportunity to join the newspaper as a photographer. She taught me how to use a camera, capture moments in time, develop film, and print images in a darkroom - skills that would empower me to be the high school photo editor, win photojournalism awards, work for a local newspaper, and help pay my way through college. If it weren't for the initial seed of photography planted by Jackie Hurt, I'm not sure I would have produced and directed four award-winning feature films.

Ironically, the older I grew, the less women became instrumental in my life.

All my sports coaches were men.
All my bosses at part-time jobs were men.
All my pastors were men.
And, almost all my professors at a Christian college were men.

Of course, my dedicated father and a number of these male leaders played powerful and unique roles in my development, but I find it interesting that *women* were so central to my early years as a human being...lessening as I got older.

How about you? As you think back over your early years, who were the women who loved you, nurtured you, and helped you learn skills that you've used for a lifetime? My guess is you have a long list.

Moving to California

During my sophomore year of high school in Kentucky, my parents began to dream about the idea of starting a church in northern California where my dad had lived during his high school years. At the time in 1989, he worked for the government and was able to secure a transfer allowing us to make the big move.

Needless to say, I was quite popular during the last two weeks of school, because I was moving to the land of beaches and babes. When we showed up in Stockton, California, I failed to write back to mention that there were no beaches (mostly cows and vineyards) or that our car stereo was stolen within the first week. Of course, this was back when people still put new stereos in their cars...and when Stockton was just recovering from being on the national news due to a schoolyard shooting.

While my dad settled in to his new job, my mom and I visited all the high schools within a 30-minute drive to find out which one had the best photo-journalism program. Ultimately, my parents bought a house in Lodi so that I could attend Tokay High School and continue my pursuit of photography. What a gift that was!

Soon after, my family and I started attending Faith Fellowship Foursquare Church on Sunday mornings. (If you're not aware, Foursquare is one of many denominations within the realm of evangelical Christianity. Think people raising their hands during worship, speaking in tongues, and being uber-friendly.) Every week, a group of teenagers would come over and say 'hello' - inviting me to join them on Wednesday night for youth group. As a slight introvert with a heavy southern accent and a six-foot-five gangly frame, this was a total nightmare. By this time, I'd made the basketball team and hanging out with these weirdos was far below me in my mind.

Eventually, I gave in and showed up on a Wednesday night, and I met two guys who were passionate about God...and not total geeks. I told the youth pastor, "I want what they have."

Pastor Rick and my two new friends gathered around me, and we prayed together. Something shifted in me that night. I'm sure there was a deeply spiritual component to it all, but more than anything, I finally felt like I was part of something bigger than myself. I felt included and accepted.

There's no better feeling than to be loved by people...people who actually want to be with you.

I spent the next year going to church and youth group soaking up as much God-stuff as I could. We worshiped, prayed, spoke in tongues, read the Bible, and went to Taco Bell...week after week.

In late December 1990, our youth group traveled to Dallas, Texas, to a giant convention for all the kids in Foursquare churches across the nation. The arena was packed with teens who were ready to be challenged to give up everything to live for God...and I was one of them. In fact, on New Year's Eve, I kneeled down on the cold floor of that arena with thousands of other kids, and I had the profound sense that I was being called into ministry as a pastor.

When I arrived home, I began to cry as I told my parents that I didn't think I should go back to Western Kentucky University to study photojournalism.

"I think I'm supposed to be a pastor," I told them.

They looked at each other and started to laugh a bit.

"We had that sense, but we didn't want to push you into it."

The Start of Something New
As I started checking out Christian colleges down the west coast and wrapping up my work on the high school yearbook, I was excited about my future. Meanwhile, I knew my dad was in conversation with our pastor about the idea of starting a new church in a neighboring town...just far enough away so it wouldn't take people away from the current church. There was discussion about it being a Foursquare church, but then there seemed to be some sort of hiccup.

As a teenager, I would hear things among the adults in passing, but I felt like I never got the full story. I heard whispers of jealousy, power struggle, rumors, and disagreement over theology.

The one thing I remember more than anything else is that my dad was unable to align with the Foursquare denomination's belief on women in leadership. Founded in 1927 by Aimee Semple McPherson, the Foursquare Church was known for empowering women to be involved and in leadership at all levels of ministry. In contrast, my dad was educated at Southern Baptist Theological Seminary where it was taught that a woman is to submit to her husband as the head of the household and is not allowed to be a pastor or elder in a local church.

Frankly, I'm not sure how all the conversations went down, but I soon found myself setting up metal chairs in a meeting hall in Galt, California, about 15 minutes up the road from our old church. Harvest Christian Fellowship started with our family and one other...as an independent non-denominational church.

Women in Leadership?
While my parents were busy with the church, I headed off to Southern California College (now called Vanguard University) to pursue a degree in pastoral ministries. During my freshman year in a church leadership class, I was assigned to write a paper on a subject of my choice. It could have been focused on evangelism, worship, discipleship, staffing, or any number of other topics, but I chose to write on *women* in church leadership.

I remember walking out of the library with a giant stack of books on the subject, and my friend asked me a very simple question.

"Why do you think this subject is such a big deal for you?"

"Huh, what do you mean?" I asked.

I was blind to the depth of my underlying struggles, but his question stuck with me.

"Why *am* I so passionate about this subject? Is it because I'm truly interested in understanding what the Bible says about women? Is it because I'm trying to reinforce my father's belief? Or, am I scared that he might not be right?"

In the process of writing that paper, I dove into quite a few books that argued multiple perspectives on the issue. For some, the literal interpretation of the Bible indicated that women could never be in a position to lead or teach men. For others who focused on the culture in which the scriptures were written, women could serve in any capacity.

I exegeted Bible passages, conducted Greek word studies, and wrestled with the topic for weeks...ultimately crafting a paper espousing that God's plan was for a man to be the leader of his wife, his family, and the church.

I got an A.

Three years later during my senior year of college, I wrote a second paper on women in church leadership. Once again, I dove into countless books arguing both sides, exegeted Bible passages, conducted Greek word studies, and crafted a paper espousing that women were actually being *liberated* in the scriptures from the patriarchal culture of the day.

What changed?
Well, it definitely wasn't the books or the Bible or the words.
It was me.

Some might say I was bending the Bible to fit my newfound perspective on life and ministry, and they probably aren't wrong. In fact, that's vastly true for anyone who reads the Bible, because it's virtually impossible for us to read anything without looking at it through the lens of our own culture and experience.

What happened to me in between those two papers?

First, I was exposed to new ways of reading the Bible by the male professors at my college who affirmed the leadership gifts of women and their calling in the local church (despite the obvious lack of female professors in the religion department).

Simultaneously, I was going to therapy to process some of my own stuff, and I started to differentiate my thoughts about life and ministry from my mom and dad. I was slowly becoming my own person.

And, most profound of all, I got married at the age of 21 to Laura, an incredibly gracious and patient woman who I deeply loved (and still do). For the first time in my life, I started to see the world a bit more through the eyes of a woman.

Don't get me wrong. I wasn't a feminist by any means.

I remember having multiple conversations with my wife about *me* being the head of the household and needing to have the final say on decisions when we absolutely disagreed. (Good lord.) Despite writing a paper with one perspective, I was having trouble living that out in my newly-formed marriage. My wife is an obvious saint.

After graduating, I desperately wanted to get hired at a church, but I didn't have any experience and asked way too many questions. Instead, I went to work in the corporate world at a paper distribution company.

Ironically, my first boss was a woman.

Over the past 25 years, I have worked with women in numerous capacities. I've been led by female pastors as a member of their staff, and I've hired female pastors when I was a lead pastor myself. As a filmmaker, I profiled six female abolitionists fighting to end sex trafficking in the United States, and as a marketing consultant, I've been hired by more female executives than male.

I've often asked my wife, "Why do I work with so many women?"

In fact, my closest friends outside of my wife are generally women.

Inspiration Rising
Since transitioning out of full-time ministry in 2008, I've had the opportunity to leverage my skills to make the world a better place in quite a few ways including producing and directing four award-winning feature films on issues that are important to our world.

In late 2018, I shared with my wife that I wanted to start making an impact on more of a daily basis than year-to-year. (My films have generally taken twelve months to produce from concept to completion.)

We talked about me starting a podcast as a platform from which to develop a coaching program that would formalize what I've been doing for 25 years...helping people get unstuck, clarify their goals, and take their lives to the next level.

INTRODUCTION

Of course, two of the first questions were, "What will the podcast be about? Who will the podcast be for?"

If a podcast is for everyone, it's for no one. There needs to be a focus, a theme, and an intended audience.

I started to think about the demographic of people most attracted to and impacted by my work. Frankly, it was obvious. From ministry to filmmaking to marketing, the people who have been most drawn to me and my efforts have been women who are 30 to 60 years old.

In 2019, Inspiration Rising was born with a desire to inspire women (and the men who support them) to rise up in life, love, and leadership. The podcast is listened to by thousands of people each week, and the Launch Your Life coaching program is empowering people to rise up in all areas of their lives.

I absolutely love interviewing women on the podcast, giving them one more platform from which to share their wisdom. I don't sense that I have an agenda to be the one who somehow rescues women or lifts them up as if I'm some sort of savior.

In fact, some people have suggested that I have an opportunity to speak out on issues of inequality, sexism, or women's rights, but I just feel like I'm supposed to help in my own way. Maybe it involves those issues at some point, but more than anything, I'm passionate about helping women cultivate a rich, meaningful life while they're here on this earth.

Of course, I want both women *and* men to live incredible lives, but there's something about the role of women in our culture that I believe is often overlooked and yet foundational.

Women nurture and sustain life.
Women manage households.
Women teach life-long skills.
Women cultivate relationships.
Women lead in unique and powerful ways.

Some would even say...women run the world!

If a woman does not embrace her true identity...
If a woman does not believe she is loved, whole, and enough...
If a woman doesn't have a powerful vision for her life...
If a woman isn't healthy in her mind, body, and soul...

her family, friends, community and the world at large are going to miss out on something that we all need.

We need women (and men) to live inspired lives!

As the Inspiration Rising community began to form, I wanted to set the tone for the type of life I longed for each person to experience. I envisioned a manifesto of sorts...a short statement that would embody all the beauty of living an inspired life.

I wrote the *Inspiration Rising Manifesto* for you.

Yes, I used the word manifesto on purpose, because a manifesto is a "public declaration of intentions." While others have sought to use this word in negative ways that have caused great harm over the years, we *can* and *must* reclaim it for a new day.

I want to give you powerful words to influence the way you *intend* to live. Yes, you heard that right. I'm seeking to influence the way you think about your life. I want you to live an inspired life, and I believe it starts with your intentions.

Would you be willing to read the Inspiration Rising Manifesto out loud?

There's something powerful that happens when we read something out loud even if we're the only one who can hear it.

Women (and men) around the globe are reading these seven sentences each morning as a way to jumpstart their day.

Let's say it together...

Inspiration Rising Manifesto

My life has been inspired from the moment of conception.
I am whole and complete just as I am.
I don't have to do or be anything else to be loved.

This is my true identity.

Embracing my inspired-ness, I am discovering my
unique way to bring inspiration to the world.
My life story, wiring, and strengths are my super powers,
and I am learning to use them with others
- for the sake of others.

I have access to all the resources I need to live out my inspiration,
and I will be strong and courageous in the face of any challenge.

My inspiration is rising.

Which phrase or sentence stood out to you?
Did anything catch you off guard?
What did you need to hear today?

I believe these words are life-changing if you'll embrace them as your own, and that's why I've written this book. Over the next nine chapters, I want to help you dig in to the concepts that are interwoven in the Inspiration Rising Manifesto in the hopes that you will...

embrace your true identity,
uncover your super powers,
and bring your inspiration to the world.

You have one life, and it's up to you how you live it.

No matter where you grew up...
No matter how your parents treated you...
No matter what setbacks you've experienced...
You are responsible for your one and only life.

EMPOWERED TO RISE

If you feel
lost,
stuck,
overwhelmed,
resentful,
depressed,
hopeless,
or just down-right tired,
I'm here to tell you...
this is not your identity, nor your future.

You can have an inspiring life full of everything you've ever dreamed...
but it starts with how you see yourself and the world around you.

Are you ready to find out who you *really* are?
Are you ready to learn who you've *always* been?
Are you ready to embrace your *true* identity?

Section 1

EMBRACING
YOUR TRUE IDENTITY

"When I talk about self-acceptance, it's not just a weight problem. It's a human problem. Everybody goes through these moments in their lives when they don't like their job or their car or their house or they don't like the way that they interact with people. I mean, how many times have you had a conversation with somebody and you go home and you beat yourself up over it? What I always talk about is getting to that place of true self-reflection. When you look at the things that you don't like, you have to figure out if you're willing to deal with the consequences of staying in that space or changing it."[1]

BEX BEDFORD
Self-acceptance champion
Body positive activist

Chapter 1

I AM INSPIRED

"My life has been inspired from the moment of conception."

Have you ever marveled at the fact that you even exist? What are the odds of you being conceived by your parents and being born into this world? Dr. Ali Binazir actually attempts to quantify the probability by calculating a number of simple factors that produce extraordinary results.[2]

First of all, what is the probability of your dad meeting your mom? Dr. Binazir estimates one in 20,000.

What's the likelihood of them staying together long enough to have kids? Through some fancy math, he estimates one in 2,000.

The combined probability is one in 40 million. Now, let's take the sperm and egg into account.

> *"You are the result of the fusion of one particular egg with one particular sperm. Each sperm and each egg is genetically unique because of the process of meiosis. A fertile woman has 100,000 viable eggs on average. A man will produce about 12 trillion sperm over the course of his reproductive lifetime. Let's say a third of those (4 trillion) are relevant to our calculation, since the sperm created after your mom hits menopause don't count. So the probability of that one sperm with half your name on it hitting that one egg with the other half of your name on it is one in 400 quadrillion."*

There you go. The chances of you existing are one in 400 quadrillion.

I know you math nerds are thinking, "Well, that's not exactly correct." Okay, sure, we can't prove all the numbers. That's why it's called probability! You get the point.

The odds that you exist at all are basically...ZERO. You are truly a miracle. From the moment of your conception, your life has been inspired!

Okay, hold off on visualizing the conception part...

Let's fast-forward to the delivery room.[3] When was the last time you actually took a moment to contemplate your arrival into the world? Even though you don't remember the actual day or the precise moment, envision your mom lying there in the hospital bed. You've seen photos of her when she was younger...before she earned all those gray hairs from the stress of worrying about you!

Can you see her face?

Perhaps *her* mother or a close friend is at her side.
Maybe your father is in the room.

Can you see the anticipation in their eyes?

They are so excited to meet you...and probably a bit nervous about your arrival. Will everything be okay? Will you have all ten fingers and ten toes?

Can you see your mom grimacing in pain with each contraction?
Do you hear the voices reassuring her?

As you make your entrance into the world, do you see the look of love on your mother's face? Can you hear your family cheer with excitement as they learn of your arrival?

If you've ever given birth...
If you've watched a child being born...
If you've held a newborn baby...
If you've looked into the eyes of a young child...
you know the absolute miracle of life.

An Extra 15 Minutes
After being married several years, Laura and I started trying to get pregnant, and month after month, the disappointing news of a period would arrive. As our friends would announce their pregnancies or send out baby shower invitations, the flow of tears would stream down Laura's face, and I would do my best to comfort her.

I AM INSPIRED

Two years later, we finally went to the doctor to see if there were any physical complications. When all the results came back as normal, Laura was prescribed a fertility drug to increase our chances of conceiving.

She was scheduled to start taking the medication on a Friday, and we found out on Wednesday that she was pregnant. I'll never forget standing in our kitchen as we embraced with tears and gazed at the double line on the pregnancy test.

We had no idea what we were in for, but we were excited nonetheless.

Eight months later, we were in a movie theatre watching *Arlington Road*, and Laura gets up to use the bathroom. As the suspense builds, I sink deep into my seat, and I hear someone whispering from behind, "David...David."

I'm thinking, "Who is God's name is interrupting me during the best part of the movie? What the..."

"David..."

I finally turned around, and I see Laura waddling down the aisle.

"My water just broke. We need to go."

"It's the last fifteen minutes of the movie...and you're three weeks early. Are you kidding me?!?!?!" (Okay, I didn't actually say that, but it's what I was thinking.)

With her pants stuffed with paper towels, we scurried out to the car, rushed home to pick up a bag, and headed to the hospital to quickly check in. Things were happening so fast, and I was about to become a father!

Standing next to Laura's bed, she gripped my hand tightly...sweating, moaning, and nervous. (I think *she* was stressed, too.)

This thing started to emerge from between her legs, and I literally said out loud, "What is *that*?"

Um, that's your daughter's head getting squeezed into the size of a large peach as it emerges from your wife's loins. (Good lord.) I saw things that day I can't unsee.

Out pops a skinny red body covered in white goopy stuff, and it was the most magical moment ever. How does this even happen? Over 12 hours after we checked in to the hospital, our daughter, Waverly, entered this world after overcoming a one in 400 quadrillion chance of being born. It's like she was covered in a glorious glitter of inspiration from the moment she arrived.

And...I'm pretty sure we could have waited an extra 15 minutes to see the end of the movie.

More Than a Feeling

You may be thinking, "Okay, sure, babies are pretty amazing, but at this stage of life, I wouldn't necessarily call *myself* inspired."

So, when exactly did your inspiration glitter wear off?
Was it when you went to school and someone made fun of you?
Was it when you liked that boy, and he broke up with you?
Was it when you tried out for that team and you didn't make it?

Was it when you failed a class, experienced abuse, were fired from a job, got a divorce, had a miscarriage, or _____?

Or, did it wear off from the day-to-day stress of life...from taking care of the kids, trying to make a relationship work, holding down a job, and making sure a location scout from the show *Hoarders* doesn't show up at your front door?

It's funny how the challenges of life can scrub away the sparkle of inspiration and leave us feeling like survival is the best case scenario. We start to believe that sparkles are for movie stars and so-called influencers who don't know what it's like to live in the real world - our world - the world where bills and baby barf and dust and dog hair are the norm.

Ok, so let's take a step back and open up the Merriam-Webster dictionary for a moment. The word *inspire* can be traced back to the Latin word *inspirare*, which means "to breathe or blow into." In its earliest written English usage, it meant "to influence, move, or guide through divine or supernatural agency or power."[4]

Unfortunately, our modern, watered-down usage has come to evoke a warm and fuzzy feeling of motivation that comes and goes based on the highs and lows of our day.

What if we started to think about inspiration as something so much more than an emotion?

What if inspiration was part of your identity...your true identity?

What if the Divine breathed inspiration into you at the moment of your conception? What if that miraculous-ness of babies is still within you? What if it never went away, but somehow you've forgotten about it or become distracted by other things?

What if you're *still* just as inspired as you were the moment you were conceived *and* the moment you arrived into this world?

Where Life Happens 24/7
Last Sunday, my family and I decided to grab lunch at a restaurant called Norms. (Imagine if Denny's and Waffle House had a baby, and it came out looking orange.) If you've heard of this iconic southern California chain of diners, your face is either smiling with delight or squished up in revulsion. There's really no in between.

Norms' slogan is "Where Life Happens 24/7", and they're not wrong.

After putting our name in and noticing a large crowd in the lobby area, we take a seat on the curb of the sidewalk as we wait for our name to be called.

A few minutes later, a woman walks up carrying a backpack and a duffel bag. She plops them down on the ground about 20 feet away from us, and asks, "Are you driving?"

"Not at the moment," I respond.

"Well, I'm lookin' for a ride down to the library."

"Which one?" I ask.

"The Mariners Library in Newport Beach."

My mind starts searching for clues...trying to figure out this woman's situation.

"You from around here?" I ask.

"Oh, I'm up here from Laguna Beach just doing some shopping."

Hmmm. Highly unlikely. She's walking down a major street that's known to attract people who are experiencing challenges in life.

I started to wonder...
Is this woman sane?
Is she really traveling?
Is it safe to be sitting this close to her?

The woman *is* rather well-kept...including her shoes and bags...two things that aren't easy to keep clean when you're living outdoors.

"Are you driving?" she loudly asks a guy exiting the restaurant.

He glances up from his phone, grunts at her awkward request, and keeps moving. She starts talking to herself, and one of my questions was partially answered.

You're probably thinking the same thing we were. Why is she asking if people are driving? What a weird question! Just ask for a ride. Geez. I feel like I want to start coaching her on how to get rides more effectively, but I'm not sure my advice would be well-received.

"Are you driving?" she politely asks a well-dressed couple in their late-70s as they walk within arm's-length of her.

The silver-haired woman wearing a black sweater with a faux fur collar turns in disgust and says, "Who would ever let *you* into their car? You pig!"

This is one of those moments when time stands still, and I wonder if I'm *actually* hearing what just entered my ears.

"You're the filthy pig!" yells the woman with two bags.

Well, that escalated quickly.

I AM INSPIRED

"Who in their right mind would ever let someone as nasty as *you* into their car?" the older lady asks again.

Okay. I think we get your point.

"You mother _____ing skank!" the ride-seeker yells.

Meanwhile, the lady's husband pinches the top of her sweater between his two fingers and slowly leads her to their ever-so-precious vehicle, and the woman asking for a ride gets in...one...more...jab.

"Your car won't even let you into...*your car!*"

Probably one of the greatest mic drop moments I've ever witnessed.

"Trotter, party of four..."

We hopped up off the curb and headed inside. I didn't catch a glimpse of their vehicle, but my guess is it was an pristine, older-model, black Cadillac with their names monogrammed on a fuzzy dashboard cover. (Oh, you were thinking that, too?)

Our lunch conversation began with the question...
  "Who says that to another human being?"

Let me answer that for you. Someone who denies the inspiration within another.

When we choose to think *less* of someone based on their...
circumstances in life,
gender,
sexual orientation,
nationality,
ethnicity,
skin color,
religion,
education,
or socio-economic status,
we have denied their true identity as one who is inspired.

I believe the inherent value of every human being is based on the fact that the Divine has breathed life into them. Each and every person is inspired, and that inspiration doesn't rub off or evaporate no matter what they experience (or don't experience).

And...that includes you, too.

If you've failed to live up to your parent's expectations (or your own)...
If you've been married and divorced (or not married at all)...
If you've lost a child (or haven't been able to have one)...
If you've been fired from a job (or can't seem to catch a break)...
If you've had to drive a clunker car (or can't even afford one)...
If you've walked away from your religion (or never even believed)...

YOU ARE STILL INSPIRED!

No matter what has happened in your life (good, bad, or ugly), you have always been inspired, because it's your *true identity*.

Your true identity is something that never changes, because it is rooted in the fact that you were breathed into life by the Divine (maybe you use words like Universe, God, Goddess, or something else). You identity isn't based on outward circumstances or even your inner thoughts and emotions. It is interwoven into the very fiber of your being.

"I am not my body. I am so much more than that," shared Ali Tate Cutler, the first plus-size Victoria's Secret model, who I interviewed on the Inspiration Rising podcast. "That's what I feel my mission here on Earth is to do, which is to help people realize that we are so much more than our bodies. And yes, body image is important to get that sorted out, to feel a sense of love about yourself at any size, because we need to transcend the body. We need to move to the higher plane of existence, which is that you are this eternal soul on this Earth, coming here with a mission. And your character and your values and your mission are so much more important than what you look like."[5]

We live in a culture where it's tempting to base our identity on what we look like, how much money we make, the level of our education, where our home is located, what kind of car we drive, the brand of clothes we wear, or even what sports team we follow.

Those things are all fine, but what if you choose to embrace your true identity...something that is rooted so much deeper...something that provides you with a firm foundation for your life?

When I was a kid, the Space Shuttle was a huge deal, and we'd always gather around to watch it take off. Of course, the spacecraft itself gets all the attention, but take a moment to think about the launchpad. I've never personally inspected it, but I've seen photos of the massive structure required to provide the Space Shuttle with a solid foundation from which to launch.

Can you imagine if the engineers at NASA chose to build the foundation out of something flimsy like sand or sticks or cardboard?

The entire thing would go up in smoke the moment the rockets ignite at lift-off. What a disaster that would be! In the same way, you and I need a solid foundation from which to launch and take our lives to the next level.

That foundation is your *true identity*.

What Sets You Apart
Because you have the breath of the Divine within you, you've been *inspired* from the moment of conception. It's what sets you apart from the trees and the rocks and the birds. I absolutely love the environment (and particularly our dog, Lexington), *but* the spirit or soul within you and me seems to be different from all that surrounds us, doesn't it?

That's where your inspiration lives.

I'm not saying the Divine hasn't breathed life into the rest of the living things around us, but there's something unique about us as human beings. We have the ability to process information, develop complex ideas, feel emotions, and chart the course of our lives with a free will.

How would your life be different if you embraced your true identity as a woman (or man) who is inspired?

What if you woke up each morning believing that your life has been inspired from the moment of conception?

What if you walked around every day knowing that you have the breath of the Divine flowing through your lungs?

What if you lived each and every moment with a confidence that you have something unique to bring to this world?

In every relationship...
In every interaction...
In every workplace...
In every organization...
you have something incredible to bring to the table,
because you are inspired.

I believe that about you.

I believe your true identity is not about your
gender,
ethnicity,
appearance,
education level,
bank account,
house,
car,
or anything else.

Your true identity...
the very foundation of your life...
is the fact that you are inspired.

The Divine has breathed life into you,
and you are good.

"I believe that your pathway to healing inevitably leads you to your soul's purpose. In that breaking down, the challenge, the stumbling blocks, and the traumas we've experienced in our life, oftentimes those are our greatest teachers and lead us to the thing that lights our soul on fire."[6]

SARAH SMALL
Holistic Business Coach and Medical Intuitive

"The brainwashing of what a woman is supposed to look like runs really deep within women. There's this shame and the should and the shadows that so many women carry about what they think they're supposed to be for the outside world. Most of what we think ends up as symptoms, so we can't just stuff our symptoms with supplements and pills and diet and exercise. It's really how we think and what we believe about ourselves that's so important."[7]

DIANE KAZER
Functional Diagnostic Nutrition Practitioner

"As introverts, we crave silence and solitude. When we're with people, we don't always feel like we have to talk. We're encouraged or we're told that you always have to have a conversation going. You've got to be social and make connections. We don't need to be having a constant conversation for us to spend time together. Just being comfortable with silence both in relationships and personally, being okay to take time away in solitude, I think that's a huge strength that introverts have."[8]

CHELSEY BROOKE
Professional Counselor and Pathfinder Coach

Chapter 2

I AM ENOUGH

"I am whole and complete just as I am."

Dressed in my black cap and gown, I sat among my fellow classmates as the commencement speaker went on and on about making a difference in the world and being focused on the right things in life. I don't remember who spoke that day, because I was focused on one thing and one thing alone.

I was waiting to hear my name called *twice*...not once like everyone else... but *two* times for *two* different degrees.

During my sophomore year of college, I became aware that I could take general education classes through what were called "tele-courses" back in the day. I enrolled at two different community colleges in order to blaze through classes that I didn't really care about.

Needless to say, I never watched the classes on the local cable access channel. Instead, I filled out the tests right before the deadlines...resulting in a low-cost, easy A, which allowed me to accumulate credits quickly. By my junior year, I was starting to take Masters level courses with the goal of graduating with my BA and MA at the same time.

"David Trotter - Bachelors in Pastoral Ministries"

As I walked across the stage, my parents and wife, Laura, were watching and cheering me on. Did I mention I was married the year before at the age of 21? Cuz, why not get married while you're in college? No sense in wasting time, right?

During my senior year of college, I was finishing both my undergraduate and graduate classwork. I was the photo editor for the school newspaper and yearbook. I was a teacher's assistant helping a professor edit his book on church leadership as well as write the discussion questions for each chapter. I was working part-time for Nabisco...stocking grocery store shelves and building end-cap displays. And...I was working on my master's thesis...all...at...the...same...time.

What the %&*@?!?!

Who in God's name does all of that? Who stretches themselves so thin... physically, intellectually, emotionally, and relationally...to try to accomplish so much in a short period of time?

Let me tell you.

Someone who doesn't feel like they are enough.
Someone who has a voice inside their head that says...

I'll never be
smart enough,
attractive enough,
spiritual enough,
pastoral enough,
strong enough,
good enough,
or man enough
to be worthy of
approval,
accolades,
attention,
support,
concern,
care,
or love.

That's who works their butt off to do all that stuff within four years.

"David Trotter - Masters in Church Leadership"

I did it. I walked across the stage twice in one day. This is where I'm supposed to tell you that it didn't feel like I thought it would, and it wasn't worth it. That's not true.

It was exhilarating. I was *the man*. I crossed the finish line twice in one day, and people were congratulating me for my accomplishment.

The only problem is that I hadn't quite broken through the finish line ribbon of the master's degree. My coursework was done, but my thesis was only 75% complete. The research questionnaires I sent out to churches were back in my possession, but I had not completed my analysis or the corresponding conclusions.

Prior to graduating, I pursued getting a job in ministry, but I had a couple of things going against me. First of all, I didn't have a track record of volunteering at the same church throughout my college years. I bounced around a lot and didn't stick it out when things felt a bit challenging. Secondly, I was very young and asked way too many questions.

With no ministry possibilities in sight, I applied to work at a paper distribution company that was opening up a new regional office near our home, and I got hired. Throughout training and during my initial months, my mind would drift toward my thesis.

What started out as mild anxiety quickly shifted to deep dread.

I was completely burned out on writing papers, and the last thing I wanted to do was re-enter the collegiate race course to finish the marathon I had already celebrated. The medals still jingling around my neck were weighing me down to the point of emotional exhaustion.

Months went by, and I finally made the call to my advisor's office.

"Hi, this is David Trotter, and I just wanted to let you know that I'm not going to finish my thesis."

That was one of the most brutal phone calls I've ever made, and it was completely liberating all at the same time.

I quit. I felt like a failure, but I also felt the relief.

On LinkedIn, all you'll see is "MA, abt." All...but...thesis. Incomplete. Not enough. Didn't finish. Loser.

Andrea Owen, author of *How To Stop Feeling Like Sh*t: 14 Habits That Are Holding You Back From Happiness*, shared with me "You wouldn't let other people talk to you the way your inner critic talks to you. And not just that, our inner critic is directly related to our core belief systems - the things we truly are committed to believing about ourselves. So, if you are beating yourself up 24/7, chances are you have a core belief that says, 'I'm not good enough. I am always a failure. I am a screw-up. I'll never be _____' (fill in the blank). We start making our decisions from that place about who we are, who our relationships are with, and what we will tolerate in our lives. You can see the chain of events that can be unleashed when we aren't speaking to ourselves kindly."[9]

Making that dreaded phone call to indicate I wasn't going to finish was a small way of breaking through and saying, "Enough already! I am enough! I don't need this stinkin' piece of paper to be pastoral enough or smart enough or anything else."

I just wanted to move on. I wanted to focus on my wife, my job, and pursuing a possible role in ministry.

The months turned into years, and I was yearning to be back in an environment of learning. Ultimately, I transferred my credits to Fuller Theological Seminary where I went on to complete a larger masters degree in cross cultural studies.

This time...my name was called once...and I actually crossed the finish line.

Where Did That Hole Come From?
When our son, Emerson, was little, he loved to play soccer out on the playground during recess, and his jeans would come home with grass stains and even holes in the knees. The conversation would undoubtedly go something like this...

"Emerson, what happened to your jeans?" asks Laura.

"Oh, I didn't even see that. Wow!" responds Emerson.

"Did you fall down?"

"No, I was just playing soccer," as he shrugs his shoulders.

"Well, those holes had to come from somewhere."

The hole of not-enough-ness has to come from somewhere, doesn't it? Some people seem to have a bigger hole in their proverbial heart than others. For some of people, you can tell them that they are _____ enough (fill in the blank with smart, attractive, hard working, etc.) all day long, and it will never sink in. For others, they seem to have an innate enough-ness already within them.

Unfortunately, many people aren't even aware that they have a hole at all. That sounds kinda funny, but you know what I mean! Have you ever met someone who is *so* driven to excel or *so* disconnected from relationships or *so* down on themselves, that they don't even realize what's going on in their life?

They haven't awakened to the possibility that there's something going on in their head and heart that's impacting the very direction of their life. They don't realize they have a black hole they're trying to fill with some sort of compensating behavior.

I turned to over-working.

Others choose
over-drinking,
over-medicating,
over-shopping,
over-exercising,
over-gambling,
over-eating,
over-controlling,
and over-_____.

Do you recognize how you might be *over-ing* in your own life?

Karen Martel, certified transformational nutrition coach, warns, "Nobody cares if you're Wonder Woman. And if they do, you don't need them in your life. Start asking for help, start taking some time off, going on vacation, doing nothing. Get over this need to pride yourself on how much you're doing in a day, because it's destroying you. We shouldn't be proud of that."[10]

Once I recognized that I was using all my academics and activities to somehow prove that I was enough, I started to naturally wonder, "Where did this hole come from?"

I believe the source of our not-enough-ness comes from three places, and some of us experience it more or less from each area. As we dive into these experiences, our focus must be on understanding and enlightenment rather than on blame. Ultimately, no matter what we've experienced in life, it is up to us to take responsibility for our response and how we choose to live from this day forward.

The first source of our not-enough-ness is usually our...

1. Home of origin

That's a fancy way of saying our parents or those who raised us. The people we spent the most time with growing up...Mom and Dad for most of us...profoundly shaped the way that we see ourselves.

From the emotional stress your mother experienced while you were still in her womb, to the facial expressions you saw on your parents' faces, to the way they talked to you and to one another... all of this impacted your identity and self-talk.

If you grew up in a home where you felt wanted, loved, and emotionally secure, you will likely have a different view of yourself than someone who grew up in a home where love was based on performance, relationships were erratic, and emotions were volatile.

While my dad worked for the government, my mom stayed at home until I was in elementary school. Both my parents were very present at school and sporting activities, with my dad even coaching a number of my teams. Although they had disagreements, I only remember them having one loud argument when I was around five years old.

They loved each other, and they loved me.
In fact, I don't remember a time when I didn't feel loved.

And yet, I started to pick up on this sense that I needed to perform in a certain way or my dad would get mad at me. Even that word *mad* feels so foreign to me, but it seems to fit in this scenario. I can still see his lips pursed in disapproval over something I was doing that was inappropriate in his eyes.

When I was a kid, we attended church in someone's home instead of a church building, and oftentimes, the kids would head back to a bedroom to play after the service. At the time, I was really into baseball cards, and I had given several of the other kids some cards as a gift. I don't remember the exact scenario, but there was a disagreement. Two of the kids took the cards I had given them, and they tore them up right in my face. I can still remember the pain of that moment.

With no prior fighting experience that I can remember, I lit into both of them with arms flailing. Within a matter of moments, my dad came tearing into the bedroom and hauled me out to the car. I remember wetting my dress pants on the way out, because I was so fearful of what my dad was going to say or do.

Spankings were not frequent, but they were part of the behavior modification strategy that my parents employed. A thin dowel rod would emerge from a hidden spot, and I knew the "this hurts me more than you" talk was about to begin.

With my pants wet and my heart broken, I was spanked for lashing out in anger. Thirty-five years later, I've raised my own kids, and I have the understanding that my dad was doing what he thought was best in the moment. What I *really* wanted was for him to hold me, hug me, and comfort the pain I was experiencing...the pain of betrayal. Instead, I picked up on the message that I needed to behave or perform perfectly in order to receive approval.

When I brought home a grade of an A-minus, the question was asked, "Why didn't you get an A?" When I brought home an A, "Wasn't there extra credit?" Some of this was in jest, but some wasn't.

Looks of disapproval, fear, and punishment are tools that parents have used since the beginning of time, because they work. They modify behavior, but they also change the heart. It hasn't been until recent years...under the nudging of my wife who has been a kindergarten teacher for most of her career...that I have come to recognize these tools as heart-breakers. They break the heart-connection between parent and child and usually result in a not-enough-ness hole that can last a lifetime if not filled in at a later point.

Your not-enough-ness story is probably different than my own, but many of us have one. This isn't about blaming my father. Heck, my kids have their own not-enough-ness story that we have un-knowingly (and knowingly) contributed to. They're already talking to therapists about their lives (and about us). In fact, I pay for it, because I want them to develop the tools that Laura and I have received through years of therapy.

It's amazing how much grace I began to develop for my own parents the moment my kids arrived on the scene and started pushing all my buttons. Despite the grace, I'm still left with a not-enough-ness hole that I need to deal with...and so do you.

2. The playground

The second source of not-enough-ness is the schoolyard play-ground or classroom or sports team or chess club or wherever you experienced the brutality of your peers. I hope you were able to avoid psychological or physical bullying, but my guess is that you got your fair share.

I was made fun of for being tall and skinny.

I was mocked for brushing back the sides of my parted-down-the-middle hair.

I was wrestled to the ground by Henry Barrett, because I was part of the sticker collection club.

I was punched in the stomach by older kids for a reason I have yet to find out.

What's up with that? Why are kids so mean? Where do they learn that? Perhaps it's simply an overflow of the negativity poured into them by adults at home, in the classroom, and throughout sports. What a brutal cycle, isn't it?

From parent/teacher/coach
to child
who becomes
the parent/teacher/coach
who passes on their not-enough-ness.

We put others down in an effort to lift ourselves up. We seek to dominate others in order to overcome our feelings of powerlessness. We make others look bad to make ourselves look better.

What would it take for the cycle to end?

3. Culture at large.

My guess is that you noticed the barrage of messages in advertising, movies, and music communicating that you are not enough unless you have/achieve/buy _____ (fill in the blank). Whether it's the latest high-tech gadget, fashion trend, fancy car, or false eyelashes, there's always going to be something that our consumer-driven culture is going to try to sell you.

Unless you live in a remote region, don't look at any media, and avoid using social media, there's very little chance of you steering clear of messaging that says you'll finally be _____ (fill in any attribute) if you have _____ (fill in anything that can be purchased).

And, of course, it starts early.

When I was a kid, it was the Sears Wishbook holiday catalog packed full of all sorts of things that I circled and starred so my parents would know what I desperately needed in life. In reality, I didn't need any of that crap. Okay, maybe the socks and underwear, but not much else.

I'm *not* suggesting that advertising is evil, but I am wanting us to increase our awareness of how marketing impacts the not-enoughness hole in our hearts.

There's a difference between...
"Ooooh, I need _____ in order to feel better about myself."
or
"Wow, they are really making _____ look pretty fancy in that advertisement, and I think I would enjoy having that."

Do you feel the difference? It's the subtle awareness of how our culture plays on the black hole of not-enough-ness in order to compel us to purchase anything and everything. And, I believe all this messaging isn't just selling us stuff...it's actually causing the black hole to get bigger.

Handcrafted By...

When I was a kid growing up in Kentucky, I had the opportunity to visit my grandparents in San Diego, and one of my favorite things to do was join my grandfather (Daddy Erp) in the garage-turned-woodshop. It was absolutely packed with every sort of woodworking tool you could imagine, and he was somehow patient enough to let me work on projects with him.

We made wooden cars, animal toys, a skateboard, and even a baseball bat with the word *Knockahoma* etched into it. During his many years in the woodshop, he made numerous pieces of impressive furniture including several still in my possession - a large oak roll-top desk, a bookcase, a bread box, and a spice box, and my parents have duplicates of these items as well. (These are cherished family heirlooms that will be handed down to my kids, but they're a bit dated now. Hopefully, that 1980s oak style comes back in before I die.)

After spending hours measuring, cutting, assembling, gluing, staining, and finishing these large professional pieces of furniture, my grandfather would pull out a wood burning tool and stamp the bottom of the piece with "Handcrafted by E. B. Trotter" - forever to be imprinted with his name.

His imprint wouldn't be placed upon the item until it was finished...whole and complete.

His imprint was a clear marker for people to know that he had spent hours meticulously crafting each item for a loved one.

His imprint was an indication that he approved of the work.

None of his furniture was ever sold. It was far too valuable to him. No one could pay enough money for the time and effort he put into each piece. In our culture, his work wouldn't be seen as commercially-viable or scalable.

Instead, it was (and is) a true gift from his hands and heart with his fingerprints all over it.

The only way that I've been able to fill that black hole of not-enough-ness is by embracing the imprint of the Divine on my life. In the same way that

I am inspired because of the breath of God within me, I have come to embrace that I am enough...only because I've been handcrafted by the Divine.

I am not enough because of the condition of my mind, body, or soul. I'm enough, because the Divine created me, and God's fingerprints are all over my life.

"Handcrafted by the Divine" is stamped on my soul, and for that reason alone, I am enough. I am whole and complete just as I am. Yes, I am still learning and growing in my skills and ability to navigate this world, but my wholeness, my completeness, and my enough-ness is my identity.

Please note that there is a difference between identity and skills.
My identity doesn't change, but my skills are always improving.

If you're going to be the partner, parent, employee, business owner, or student that you want to be, it begins by being clear about your identity. In fact, if you want a strong foundation, your identity won't be built on any of those roles.

Roles can change, but your identity doesn't need to when it's rooted in the fact that you were handcrafted by the Divine.

Maybe it's my background as a pastor or maybe I've become a little woo-woo, but the only thing that I've been able to find that fills the not-enough-ness hole is embracing an identity bigger than something I can manufacture on my own.

My academic degrees,
my role as a lead pastor,
my four feature films,
my wife and kids,
or anything else that I've been able to create, accomplish, or build pales in comparison to being "enough" in the eyes of the Divine.

And, for that reason, I'm banking on the fact that...
My life has been inspired from the moment of conception.
I am whole and complete just as I am.

"Unconditional love requires true love. It requires that we love in all conditions. This idea that I need to be thinner or more successful or have more money or get the guy before I can love myself is ridiculous stuff that we as humans tell ourselves. It starts with loving yourself in all conditions. Now that's true love."[11]

DR. SHANNON GULBRANSON
Author of *Date Yourself Well: The Bestselling 12 Engagements of Becoming the Great Lover of Your Life*

Chapter 3

I AM LOVED

"I don't have to do or be anything else to be loved. This is my true identity."

A long flowing mane of golden curly hair cascades down her back. The color of her hot pink shorts pops against her sun-kissed skin. Her bright smile lights up the night sky.

"Who is this new girl?" I wonder.

I had just returned for my sophomore year of college, and the fifth floor guys are gathering with our sister floor for a mixer of sorts...namely tag! When you're at a Christian college, the mixers are more like kindergarten games, but I had no problem with that.

"Okay, everyone! Girls hide and guys seek! 10, 9, 8, 7..."

As our sister floor takes off running and scatters across the campus, I'm only interested in finding one girl. I don't know her name, but there's something different about her...something magnetic.

I searched high and low that night, and I never was able to find her. Come to find out, she was a transfer student who was starting her junior year, and her name was Laura.

When I discovered that her roommate cut hair for some of the guys on my floor, I thought this might be the perfect opportunity to make the connection I missed out on during that game of tag. One night during "open hours" (when guys were allowed to be in the girls' dorm as long as doors were left open at least the length of a Bible), I headed up to the fifth floor to have my hair cut...and Laura just happened to be there.

"Well, well, well. Isn't this a coincidence!"

43

It sounds a bit stalkerish in retrospect, but I prefer to think of it as mere strategery. Everything was going great until it came time for me to pay her roommate when I realized I hadn't brought my wallet or any money. Laura immediately offered to spot me the $10, and then it hit me...

"What if I pay you back by taking you out to dinner?" I suggested.

"Sure! That sounds great."

My heart almost leaped out of my chest as I bounded down five flights of stairs.

Within days, Laura and I headed down to Newport Beach for dinner at Red Onion...never mind that it turned into Hooters a few years later...and we enjoyed a slow walk on the beach afterwards. We went out every single night for three weeks straight, and I couldn't get enough of her.

Somehow, after three weeks of dating, I thought it would be wise to tell Laura that I loved her and was going to marry her.

Yeah, that went over about as good as you'd expect.

Was it *really* love...or simply hormones...or a deep desire to connect with another human being...to want and be wanted?

Two and half months later, I got down on one knee and asked for her hand in marriage, and for some crazy reason, she said, "Yes!"

That was over 27 years ago, and my understanding and experience of love is quite different now.

Did I love Laura then? Absolutely.
Do I love her differently now? Of course.

When we started dating, I would go out of my way to express my love in any way I could...from washing her car to buying thoughtful gifts to planning special dates. I was *doing* everything I could to express my love...and earn hers.

How much of it was a desire to *express* my love versus an effort to *earn* her love? Probably a mixture, and that's okay. Relationships are obviously a give and take, and at 20 years old, I was just happy that someone wanted to be with me.

To be honest, my journey in understanding love has been far more challenging in the area of *receiving* versus *giving*.

When we started going to premarital counseling, our therapist told Laura, "David is quite an insensitive person, but when he finally sees a need, he's one of the most compassionate and loving people in the world."

And...that's true.

I'm direct, intense, and to the point...less so now than when I was 20. But, if I have a friend or family member or even a stranger in need, I will do everything in my power to help. *I just can't help it.* I will bend over backward out of my genuine desire to love and care for them.

And yet, when my wife says, "I love you,"
I will often think to myself, "But why?"

On occasion, I've even asked her out loud, and she responds with, "Are you kidding me? Stop thinking that way!"

I cognitively know that she loves me, but my challenge is *feeling* that love and knowing it deep within. That has nothing to do with her ability to love and more about my own journey of embracing love from anyone.

The question is...why would someone want to love me when I have so many challenges? Why would someone want to be with me and care about me when I have so many imperfections and flaws and issues?

Ah...the assumption is that I must be perfect in order to be lovable, and that's why this part of the Inspiration Rising Manifesto is so difficult and so important to me.

"I don't have to do or be anything else to be loved. This is my true identity."

Part of my journey as a human being (and a husband) is to embrace that I am loved, not based on performance, but as part of who I am.

My faith background has a core belief that God is love and even before God made the world, God loved us and chose us.[12] How does that all work? I'm less sure now than I've ever been, but I do know that Love is the ethic from which life is best lived. If the Divine is the source of love...the embodiment of love...and I have been created by this Source, my identity is formed by this same love.

Ironically, my name, David, means *beloved* or "one who is dearly loved." Not only am I beloved, but so are you...so is everyone. Every single human being is beloved, and we have the opportunity to embrace our beloved-ness.

You may be thinking, "I'm not sure. There are a lot of evil people in the world. Can we really say everyone is loved at their core?"

There is definitely a difference between our identity as "one who is loved" and our skills in living out that love in our daily lives.

Going Back to Kindergarten

I often think I need to go back to kindergarten when it comes to this kind of love, and luckily, I live with a kindergarten teacher who is an expert in her field. I'm not sure if you've ever spent any time with 24 little ones in a classroom, but it's controlled chaos. Five- and six-year-olds are full of energy and life and absolute craziness!

Within the first week of school, I know the names of the kids I'll be hearing about for the entire year. These are the ones who are struggling with behavior more than academics. Some are probably having a challenging experience at home, and it's playing out in the classroom and on the playground. Others may be lacking life skills, and their parents are struggling to find ways to help them. And yet, others are just adjusting to a structured environment, since they didn't go to preschool.

You may remember back to your days in elementary school when some of your teachers made statements like...

> *"Stop that!"*
> *"What's wrong with you?"*
> *"Didn't you hear me the first time?"*
> *"Shut your mouth!"*

Granted, if you locked me in a classroom with 24 five- and six-year-olds, you might hear something worse come out of my mouth. Visions of *Kindergarten Cop* come flooding to mind!

In an effort to control a classroom, color-coded behavior charts resulting in punishments or prize boxes are often used to coerce children to fall in line. Some kids have a demeanor that works within this system easily, and others really struggle. If and when a teacher labels a kid as a *problem child* and uses language that reinforces this identity, how will the child likely respond? If *you* were constantly told to "stop being bad" or "quit being a disruption", how would you feel? How would you react?

The truth is...when a teacher sees a child as a problem,
the child will likely meet that teacher's expectations.

The same is true with ourselves. If you see yourself as unlovable, unwanted, not enough, a problem, or the black sheep, you will most likely live your life based on that identity. Not only are those thoughts swirling around in your mind, but they'll impact your work, marriage, friendships, and health.

Over the years, I've watched my wife radically shift her approach to teaching by focusing on *connection before correction*. My wife was never a mean teacher. In fact, she's one of the nicest ones you'll ever meet, and parents jockey to find ways to get their kids into her classroom. Yet, she realized that some of her classroom management techniques were reinforcing behaviors in a way that wasn't working long-term for students.

At the beginning of each year, she helps the students envision their classmates as a family where everyone is loved and learning how to love. The focus is on positive behavior and the most helpful way of regulating their bodies and emotions. She's finding that when a child feels loved, seen, and safe, they more quickly develop the skills needed to flourish as a member of the class family.

Those two things go hand in hand. As we embrace our identity as one who is loved, we simultaneously have the opportunity to develop the skill of loving others.

What Exactly Is Love?
We use the term love rather loosely these days, don't we? I love fried chicken. I love my dog. I love God. I love you. Is there any difference between all

47

these different loves? In English, it ends up sounding pretty similar, doesn't it? Think for a moment about the nuances of the love we give and receive.

- **Family Love** - You've heard the saying, "Blood is thicker than water." This is an ancient proverb that means familial bonds will always be stronger than bonds of friendship or romance. There is a unique and powerful love that ties families together, and I especially see this in the lives of my Asian and Latino friends whose family bonds are beyond what I can even imagine.

- **Friendly Love** - I realize every family is different, and it's become popular to have a "chosen family" when our home of origin has been abusive, alienating, or challenging. Whether you'd call your friends your "framily" or not, the love we have for our friends can feel different. Perhaps your friends know things about you or have had experiences with you that your family knows nothing of.

- **Hospitable Love** - There are many opportunities in life when we may not be family or friends with someone, but we can show them love through hospitality. While this is traditionally expressed in the context of one's home, you can show hospitality by generously welcoming, hosting, and entertaining anyone in *any* context. Whether it's the first moment you meet or when you're having a business luncheon, a love for others can be exhibited through generous words, generous gestures, and generous listening.

- **Sexual Love** - The intimate experiences between lovers and the words shared in these tender and passionate moments create a bond like no other. There's a soul connection when we allow someone to see us and we see someone else in the most vulnerable of moments. It's a seeing beyond the physical realm...into the soul.

- **Self Love** - The way we love ourselves is unique from all the others. How you see yourself, the way you talk to yourself, and the manner in which you treat your mind, body, and soul equal your love for self. For many of us, this may be one of the most challenging ways in which to express and receive love.

- **Divine Love** - In ancient Greek, the term for this type of love was *agape*, and it was regularly used to describe the highest form of love... the love of God for humankind. C.S. Lewis writes, "Agape is the highest level of love known to humanity: a selfless love that is passionately committed to the well-being of others."[13] This love is an unconditional love that transcends mere circumstance and goes beyond momentary emotion. It is a deep abiding love.

I'm inviting you to try on this Divine love...an unconditional love...that would form your very identity...your true identity.

Rumi, a 13th century poet and Sufi mystic, is quoted as saying, "We are made of Love and made to Love."

Think for a moment about your own life. If I tell you that you don't have to do or be anything else to be loved, what's your natural response?

I start to wiggle in my seat and think, "Yeah, but..."

You are loved, and you can't fight it. Sure, you can choose not to believe it, but you'll miss out on an intimate connection with those around you.

No matter if your parents approve of your choices...
No matter what you think about yourself...
No matter the size or shape of your body...
No matter if you got the promotion or not...
No matter if he/she chooses to stay or go...
No matter if you ever live up to your potential (whatever that means)...

YOU ARE LOVED.
That's your true identity.

If you choose to live from a place where you believe you're *not* loved, then you'll strive for love, prove yourself for love, manipulate for love, and even pay or be paid for love.

When you embrace that you are loved no matter what...

You will be courageous to love yourself.
You will be focused on seeing the good in others.
You will be open to loving those who are different than you.
You will recognize that you are connected to all of humanity.

The Power of Your True Identity

In early 2008, I found myself so tired and weary from workaholism that I was unwilling to take a close look at the foundation upon which I was building my life. Rather than examining those places that were cracked and even disintegrating, I loaded the rocket of my life on the launchpad and blew the whole thing up by making some incredibly poor choices. I didn't want to do the hard work of reflecting on my identity...I simply wanted to start over.

The truth is you can't just *change* jobs or homes or spouses and find a new you. You (and all your same issues) end up going right along into that so-called new life. The old you is now in new circumstances, and the same challenges will appear once again.

When I had my own rock-bottom experience, I was finally motivated to start doing the inner work of embracing my true identity rather than compensating for my insecurities through performance, people-pleasing, and workaholism. As I continue to accept that I am already inspired, enough, and loved, I feel more grounded and centered than ever. I can celebrate my own growth, and I don't feel jealous of the success of others. I choose to serve people out of a heart of abundance rather than trying to prove my own self-worth. Is it a lifelong journey? Of course! But I'm growing, and I can feel the difference.

20 Powerful Statements Embracing Your Divine Imprint

I want to invite you to try on something that has helped me embrace my true identity. It may feel a bit unfamiliar at first, but I believe it has the ability to provide you with a grounding that is needed to launch your life. Below you will find twenty powerful statements that are part of your true identity and based on the Divine love that surrounds you and is within you.

Would you be willing to read them aloud?

I was created by the Divine.
I am loved by the Divine, family, and friends.
I have the ability to love the Divine and others.
I have a unique purpose in this world.
I am extraordinarily gifted and talented.
I am attractive in my own unique way.
I am being transformed every day.
I can learn from my mistakes.

I can have hope, peace, and joy.
I can have wisdom and understanding.
I can make healthy decisions.
I am strong and courageous.
I can find grace and mercy when in need.
I am part of a community that cares.
I am significant and exceptional.
I am not limited by other's opinions.
I have access to all the resources I need.
I have been created to make an impact.
I can anticipate greatness in my future.
I have an incredible life.

How did that feel? I realize your mind may have fought you on a couple of the statements, and that's okay. "Oh, that's not true. That one doesn't apply to me." Just try it on. Could it be true? Would others think it's true? What if I told you that I believe it's true about you?

Now, I want to invite you to read the same statements, but put your name in the blank. *And, once again, read them out loud.*

_____ was created by the Divine.
_____ is loved by the Divine, family, and friends.
_____ has the ability to love the Divine and others.
_____ has a unique purpose in this world.
_____ is extraordinarily gifted and talented.
_____ is attractive in ____ own unique way.
_____ is being transformed every day.
_____ can learn from ____ mistakes.
_____ can have hope, peace, and joy.
_____ can have wisdom and understanding.
_____ can make healthy decisions.
_____ is strong and courageous.
_____ can find grace and mercy when in need.
_____ is part of a community that cares.
_____ is significant and exceptional.
_____ is not limited by other's opinions.
_____ has access to all the resources ____ needs.
_____ has been created to make an impact.
_____ can anticipate greatness in ____ future.
_____ has an incredible life.

My guess is that felt a bit different. There's something about saying (and hearing) your own name that transforms the soul. That's what that awkward feeling was...your soul trying on your true identity.

I realize it might feel awkward at first, but keep trying it on.
It looks good on you, and it will feel good, too.

Section 2

UNCOVERING
YOUR UNIQUENESS

"Does everyone have a purpose? According to the research, we will never know. We can't scientifically know that. What we do know is people who identify as having purpose are happier and have higher life satisfaction. They're more resilient to challenges. They are more optimistic and better able to overcome. So, that's what we know. Does everyone have purpose? I personally believe that we do."[14]

CARIN ROCKIND
Creator of PurposeGirl

Chapter 4
I HAVE A UNIQUE VISION

"Embracing my inspired-ness, I am discovering my unique way to bring inspiration to the world."

"I think I'm supposed to be a flower farmer," confessed Jacqui. "But, that kind of thing is for *other* people...not for people like me."[15]

At the time, Jacqui was a mindset coach for a highly successful online medical program, but there was something missing. For most of her life, she had been the one to take care of others. From raising kids to working at a church to even moving both of her parents into the home she shared with her husband, she was gifted at nurturing others in a beautiful way.

Yet, the weight of caring for her aging parents and the fact that they passed away just one day apart caused Jacqui to turn inward into a season of grief and healing. Two years later, she began to sense that something needed to change. She needed a fresh vision for her life, so she enrolled in Launch Your Life, a coaching program we offer through Inspiration Rising.[16]

When she started the program, Jacqui wondered if becoming a death doula, someone who assists in the process of dying, could be her next step. In one of our early mastermind video calls, I tried to break the tension of the moment by joking that www.ILoveDyingPeople.com was available for purchase, and she better jump on it. She laughed...but I wasn't totally kidding. I'm always looking for ways to help people stand out from the crowd!

A few weeks later in the program, I led students in a visualization to help unearth the vision that I believe is already within them, and Jacqui reported her experience at our next mastermind video call.

"I love flowers. I love the beauty of them. I love growing and learning and getting my hands dirty," she said as she described her vision of becoming a flower farmer.

Not only did she share the vision with us that night, but she shared it with her husband, Billy.

"That's not something I could do. That's for other people," she resisted.

"Why not?" he asked. "Why can't you become a flower farmer?"

Instead of pointing out all the potential challenges or making fun of her vision, Billy actually encouraged her to nurture this idea to see where it might lead. Jacqui soon started researching various flower varieties and ended up purchasing a handful of dahlia tubers, flower roots similar to bulbs.

With the tubers sitting in a box on her back patio in preparation for planting, Jacqui noticed a man across the street who she had never seen. It turned out that he was the landlord of the adjacent property, but he wasn't around that much. Jacqui invited him over for a cup of coffee, and as he was leaving, he noticed the box.

"What are those?" he asked.

"Oh, those are tubers. I'm a flower farmer," she confidently told him.

"Wow! I'm a flower farmer, too!" he said.

What are the chances? Within a few days, this man brought over 211 tubers (at a value of $5-10 each) to give to Jacqui to help her get started!

I asked her, "If you would have known he was a flower farmer, would you ever have said you were one, too?"

"I doubt it, but I was just trying it on to see how it felt," she admitted.

There's something powerful that happens when we cultivate a vision, start taking steps in that direction, and try on what it will feel like. The Universe responded to Jacqui's faith-filled steps by providing abundantly.

Not only did this man give her over $1,000 in tubers, but he shared his knowledge with her and will be a resource as she gets started.

Identifying Your Current Path

Maybe you relate to that feeling Jacqui had...a feeling of wanting more out of life...like there's something missing. Instead of genuinely searching within ourselves to find what we want, we often fall into a groove that someone else carved out in front of us.

Michelle Coops, founder of Be a Brand Rebel, shared, "Being a rebel is not about being stubborn or going against society and all its rules. It's about finding your own way. It's all about finding that path that defines you and the path that fits the way that you want to live your life. I like to inspire people to follow their own path a little bit more, and that's why instead of just being rebellious, I call it rebelicious."[17]

Several common paths we unknowingly take include...

- The path of our parents - taking on their values and desires for our life.

- The path of our friends - embracing what they think is best.

- The path of our idol/mentor - following someone we look up to.

- The path of our culture - going along with the prevailing aspirations of our world.

Although none of these paths are unhealthy or bad in and of themselves, we end up losing part of our unique vision for life by simply following someone else. Our choices will be shaped more by what others want for our lives rather than what is developing deep within us.

Management consultant and author W. Edwards Deming writes, "Every system is perfectly designed to get the result that it does."[18]

This is not only true about an organization, but it's true about our lives.

You life is perfectly designed to get the results you're getting right now! From your relationships to physical health to income to emotional well-being, your experience of life is a direct result of how you've chosen to live and respond in this world. The truth is that you are where you are...because of what you want out of this life. You were motivated in such a way to make decisions that have gotten you to this point in time.

Of course, there are some of us who have experienced abuse, tragedy, or hardship that was completely out of our control. I'm not insinuating that those things occurred in your life (or mine) because of decisions we directly made. Yet, in response to those experiences, we often take on a victim mentality, which handicaps us from moving forward with healthy intentions.

Whether you were abused, cheated on, fired unjustly, or wrongfully accused of something, the way you respond says a great deal about what you want in this life. You and I can embrace a view of ourselves that says...

> *"I deserve the bad things that come my way."*
> *"I shouldn't ever expect good things to happen to me."*
> *"People can't be trusted, and they're always out to get me."*

Ultimately, the things you focus on create the intentions that define the trajectory of your life. It is this trajectory that determines how you'll spend your time and what goals you'll set for yourself.

Take a moment to pause and reflect. Who or what has most influenced your life's trajectory or path? And, are you willing to take responsibility for the current results in your life? Why or why not?

The Power of "What If?"
Two of the most powerful words in the world are "what" and "if." When you are courageous enough to put them together to form a simple question, possibilities start to unfold.

What...if?

I'm not talking about asking that question as you look in the rear view mirror of life...such as...what if I wouldn't have gotten married, had kids, taken that job, made that decisions, or whatever you may regret?

I'm talking about asking a powerful two-word question as you encounter your current life and envision your future. Ask that question in the midst of any problem, and solutions will start to appear. You can ask it when there's a void of resources or leadership, and amazing things start to play out. There's something about that question that allows human beings to open up the locked places within our brains. It forces us out of what we've known and into a sphere of 'un-knowing' where possibilities are endless.

If you're going to rise up in all aspects of your life, the power of possibilities will be one of your greatest assets. You'll need to have an open mind and heart to what is possible in situations that seem like a big mess and have little chance of turning around.

Think about your family and friends. What's the condition of your relationships? Are your kids functioning as part of the family unit or just doing their own thing? Do you enjoy being together or are you merely roommates? What do you see?

How about your job? Are you just in it for the money, or is there a deep passion? Would you rather be doing something else, but you're just too scared to make a move? Or, are you even aware of what you're passionate about? Think about other areas of your life…like your physical health, life partner, spirituality, and finances. What do you see?

I see possibilities.

What if you could experience a deep passion for life?
What if you could have an intensely intimate relationship with a partner?
What if you were surrounded by friends who supported and loved you?
What if you had plenty of finances to enjoy and share with others?
What if you could express yourself creatively and playfully?
What if you were physically healthy and fit?
What if you sensed a closeness with the Divine?

What's holding you back from envisioning those things for your life? Do you start to make excuses about why you don't deserve it or how it could never happen or how someone or something is holding you back? Is it possible that all those excuses have allowed you to be complacent in life and play it safe?

Stacey Robbins, author, speaker, and retreat leader, shared with me, "I think of risk-taking as inviting chaos via inspiration. Rather than waiting for life to come and slap us across the face, when I take a risk, what I'm saying is, "What inspires me is worth having in my life." It's worth going through the difficulty of facing my worst fears about it. The inspiration will be the greater vision that I have that will allow me to get to work through those fears and issues and stories, so that I can live a life that's at a higher level and a deeper joy and more aliveness."[19]

What Will It Take?

With 211 tubers now in hand, Jacqui knew there was no way that her tree-covered property outside of Portland would have enough space to plant the flowers. She immediately called her sister who lived 30 minutes away to see if she'd be willing to allow Jacqui to grow the flowers on her property, and her sister said yes!

Within days, Jacqui and Billy were tilling up the soil and planting rows of dahlia tubers for an initial test-run of her newfound vision. Soon, little green sprouts started shooting up from the ground, and Jacqui's vision started to bloom.

The only challenge was that her sister's property was 30 minutes away, and the ability to expand the number of rows was limited. Within one planting, Jacqui's vision had already outgrown the space.

If she was going to allow the vision to lead her, she needed to expand her mindset about what was possible and what resources were needed. This is the point at which many of us shrink back and stay small.

"I don't know what to do next."
"I don't have enough money."
"I don't have enough time."
"I don't have the right education or skills."

What if it was possible to learn what to do next? What if you opened yourself up to learning from others and pursuing knowledge through research online? What if you sought creative solutions that reduced costs or generated financial resources? What if you restructured your time to invest in your vision? What if you invested in training or coaching to get you where you want to go?

Knowing that her vision required more land, Jacqui and Billy could have settled for what was easy or small....a few flowers on the back porch and a dream that would ultimately go to the grave. Instead, they made a plan.

While they prepared their beloved family home for sale, Jacqui started searching for nearby property. No, it wasn't easy. Not only did it mean fixing up a few things around their current house, but it required them to process the idea of letting go of something incredibly special.

They put their heart into renovating that home.
They raised children there.
They cared for Jacqui's parents until their final days.
They made countless memories.

And yet, a vision was calling them to leave behind what was...for what could be.

Within weeks, Jacqui came across a property that had been left to sit for years after the matriarch of the family passed away. Yes, the house needed quite a bit of work, but it was perfect in all the right ways...a large two-story farmhouse, a huge barn, another smaller barn, and 6.5 acres of flat land to plant thousands of dahlias.

"What if we hosted a flower festival? What if we hosted photo shoots and events against the backdrop of the flower fields? What if we created a subscription program for people who wanted flowers delivered weekly?"

Their house sold, they bought the property, and Jacqui and Billy moved in to the farmhouse as they continue to renovate. This spring, tubers will go in the ground, and her vision will begin to blossom. While the vision may have been birthed in Jacqui's heart, it has required an intense amount of teamwork to get this far. Not only has her husband been incredibly supportive to the point of doing a great deal of physical labor and renovation, but her brother has invested countless hours as well.

Starting With the End in Mind
As many of us post our thoughts with a mere 280 characters on Twitter or a few more on Facebook or Instagram, the reality is that the whole of your life will come down to even fewer characters on your tombstone or the little plaque on your box of ashes.

Have you ever thought of life that way? Your entire life will come down to just a few words. Oftentimes, the best place to begin a new vision for your life is with the end in mind. I want to invite you to take a moment and envision your funeral and work your way back to the current day. Allow your mind's eye to travel through time.

As your casket is positioned in the front of the chapel or at the graveside, who do you see walking up on the scene? Who seems to be missing? What are they saying to one another? As people stand up to share their memories of you, what are they talking about? How do they remember you?

As you allow your mind to travel back in time, what are you doing on your final days? Who is gathered around your bed? What's happening? What are you saying to them?

How did you spend the last weeks and months of your life? What was important to you? How were you spending your time and money?

What about the last year of your life? Do you think you knew it was your last 365 days? How were you living life? How were you treating others?

Keep making your way back in time...all...the...way...back...to the current day. Now, turn around and look forward into the future toward your death. Are you happy or sad with what appeared in your mind's eye? Would you rather have seen something different? If your life stayed on its current path, what do you think people would say about you at your funeral? Are you good with that? Why or why not?

What do you want your tombstone or plaque to say? Unless you leave it in your will, your family members will decide for you. What do you want them to have engraved?

Call me morbid, but I love funerals. Of course, I'm not happy when anyone passes away (especially if I knew them), but there's nothing more sobering than the end of someone's life. In my time as a pastor, I conducted numerous memorial services where I came alongside families in their moment of loss and grief.

It is an absolute privilege to be invited into those precious moments of processing loss and beginning the grieving process. It's in those moments that everyone, including me, is reminded that life is fragile and short.

We will *not* live forever.
You and I will both pass away.

We can ignore that reality, or we can take it to heart. We can use those sobering moments to ask ourselves life-clarifying questions. This tenderness can clear away the extraneous nonsense of life and call us to focus on things that matter...things like relationships and legacy.

The question is...what do you want to be known for?

I Want A New Life

When I hit rock bottom in 2008, I found myself curled in the fetal position on the kitchen floor and unable to cope with the mess of my life. One minute, I was acting fine, and the next, I was an absolute mess.

After three dysfunctional days, my therapist and several close friends tried to talk me into going to a hospital...a mental hospital.

"That's for people who can't handle life," I protested through tears.

After having a complete meltdown in front of my four-year-old son on the way to Disneyland, I finally came to the conclusion that I couldn't handle life anymore. I dropped him off with Laura and drove straight to the hospital.

It was utterly humiliating, but exactly what I desperately needed. Half of the people in there were professionals who had breakdowns, and the other half...are probably still there.

After my anxiety started to stabilize, I called a friend asking for a giant sheet of paper and a marker. I loved charting out organizational strategies on those oversized sticky notes, and I knew my life needed some serious reorganization.

I drew a line across the top and a line down the center. On the top left, I scribbled Old Life, and on the top right, New Life. I wrote down all the things I didn't like about my *old* way of living, and I wrote the corresponding *new* way of living that I was desperate to experience.

From being stressed out all the time...to peaceful in all situations.
From being a workaholic...to resting and rejuvenating.
From being disconnected from family...to enjoying the moment.
From being roommates with my wife...to having an intimate partnership.
From being driven by ego...to serving the people around me.

All those things in the right column seemed like a world away, but it's what I wanted deep inside. It wasn't until I had everything else stripped away from my life that I was able to see what truly mattered to me.

I was starting to cultivate a new vision.

I don't want you to get to that point. It's one of the reasons why I help women (and men) through the Launch Your Life coaching program. I don't want you to have to hit rock bottom to pursue the life you truly want. I want you to have clarifying conversations *now* instead of wasting your life away or making a decision that you'll later regret.

One of the greatest challenges is when we try to live out our dreams and goals without first embracing our true identity. In my case, I sensed at age 16 that I would make a significant impact on the globe during my lifetime, and I saw that in the context of ministry. For over a decade, I strived to make that impact by growing a church as large as I could.

Was I helping people? Sure.
Were my motives clouded by ego? Absolutely.

Unfortunately, the lies I believed about "not being enough" and "people not liking me" were fueling my efforts to grow a church bigger and bigger. The truth is that's a black hole that can never be filled.

If you're not aware of the lies you are prone to believe, these dark thoughts will drive you to make decisions that will negatively impact your relationships and ultimately limit your vision in life.

That's why I'm so passionate about helping you embrace your true identity.

When you embrace (and continue embracing) the fact that you are *already* inspired, enough, and loved, your vision will flow from a place of abundance, rather than an effort to fill up the black hole of brokenness, pain, or lack. This is not a one-time event. I'm constantly reminding myself of the truth of who I am in light of my Divine origin. That's why I wrote the Inspiration Rising Manifesto and this book. It's as much a reminder for me as much as it is a gift to you.

I HAVE A UNIQUE VISION

Envisioning A Mental Picture

Jacqui's vision is not your vision. Even if you happen to think that being a flower farmer is in your future, your way of living that out will be distinctly different than hers. Why? Because we each have a unique vision.

A *vision* is a mental picture of your preferable future.

First of all, it's a *mental* picture. When you close your eyes and allow your mind's eye to see into your future, what do you see?

It may be a new job, home, or even country.
It might be a shift in the quality of your family's relationships.
Maybe it's about your health or finances or marriage or a side hustle.

Each mental picture is unique...not greater than or less than another. It is a snapshot in time that embodies your preferable future...what you truly want to experience in life.

Kelsey Murphy, business and life coach, shared with me, "As I got older, I realized that I really like my career and working - not just a hobby on the side. I wanted a successful career where I was bringing in a solid amount of finances, and I felt really proud of it. It was a thing where if I wanted to, I could fly somewhere for a girls weekend away and have a glass of champagne and feel really good about this multi-faceted life that I wanted. I had always heard that you can only have one or the other. You could be a stay-at-home mom or you can have a really successful career, and I just never really bought into that."[20]

Some of us quit dreaming long ago, and it takes time to allow our hearts to break free from the hopelessness that things will never change. That's why the question "what if?" is so important. Those two words start to massage our heart back into a state of dreaming. If that's where you find yourself, keep asking "what if?" in all aspects of your life. Slowly, you will start to dream again, and a vision will come through your heart and into your mind's eye.

When you close your eyes, what do you see?

I'm not talking about goals. I'm talking about a vision...a snapshot in time that embodies what you truly want.

Where are you?
What tools or objects surround you?
What are you wearing?
Who is with you?
What are you doing?
What are you saying?

How will you feel when this vision comes to fruition?

See it clearly.
Feel it deeply.

In this moment, you're discovering your unique way to bring inspiration to the world. The world needs what's in your heart and becoming even more clear in your mind's eye. Don't cross the finish line of life without bringing your vision into existence.

We need you.

Chapter 5

I HAVE REAL-LIFE SUPER POWERS

"My life story, wiring, and strengths are my super powers."

"Gathered together from the cosmic reaches of the universe here in this great Hall of Justice are the most powerful forces of good ever assembled...

Superman!
Batman and Robin!
Wonder Woman!
Aquaman!
And the Wonder Twins - Zan and Jayna - with their space monkey - Gleek!

Dedicated to truth, justice, and peace for all mankind!"

In the 70s and 80s *way* before YouTube or Cartoon Network or even VHS tapes, most kids were glued to the Saturday morning cartoons, and my absolute favorite was SuperFriends. Please do yourself a favor and YouTube an episode to experience the pure exhilaration of watching super heroes band together to take down the Legion of Doom.

Every one of the SuperFriends had a distinct set of powers, and when they worked together, they were unstoppable!

Superman could fly beyond the Earth's atmosphere, blow away any problem with his powerful lungs, see through virtually anything with his x-ray vision, and take down the bad guys with his super-human strength.

Batman and Robin used their incredible intellect, martial arts capabilities, detective skills, and all sorts of fancy devices on their utility belts.

Wonder Woman flew around in her invisible jet, deflected bullets with her magic bracelets, and caught criminals with her magic lasso that compelled them to tell the truth.

Aquaman could breathe underwater, communicate telepathically with sea life, and ride his giant seahorse to get places even faster.

The Wonder Twins were alien siblings who could transform when they touched fists. "Wonder Twin powers, activate!" Zan could morph into any form of water, and Jayna could transform into any animal. Of course, their space monkey Gleek was along for the ride as their comedian sidekick.

Undoubtedly, at some point in your life, you've had a friend ask you, "If you could have one super power, what would it be?" Saying "I want to be invisible" always sounded creepy to me, so I always opted for the ability to fly. Maybe that's why I have so many flying dreams!

Over the years, I've come to realize we *all* have super powers, but many of us don't even realize it or don't choose to embrace them. You may have been taught that it was prideful to celebrate your strengths. Or, maybe you were told that everything needed to be about God, and you were nothing or of no good. The truth is that our world is in desperate need of the super powers within you.

In the Launch Your Life coaching program, we define super powers as the unique combination of your life story, strengths, and wiring that are used to bring your vision to the world.

You are not an ordinary person. In fact, there are no ordinary people. Every single person on this planet is extra-ordinary, but we must be intentional about cultivating the super powers within us. Before we dive in to the different types of super powers that each of us have, I want to challenge you to...

1. **Embrace that everyone has super powers...including you.**
   Even if you're not sure what your super powers are, start by simply embracing the fact that every human being has them. There's something unique about each person. We can all agree on that, right? This uniqueness, when leveraged with intentionality, can be an incredible source of strength. There are things you can do in a matter of minutes that might take someone else days! These aren't alien talents. These are a unique real-life super powers that have been honed...even if you haven't been aware of what you've been doing.

Lisa Cummings, founder of Lead Through Strengths, shared with me, "You already have super powers in you. You already have things that come to you naturally - how you think, how you feel, how you act. If you decide to obsess over developing those, the high leverage that you get is really amazing. It actually feels easy to become better at your performance. Whereas, if you decide to obsess over your weaknesses, it's frustrating. It's draining. It makes you procrastinate, and it's a pretty depressing way to live a life and a career."[21]

2. Choose to courageously explore your real-life super powers.
I realize it might feel a little awkward for some of us to reflect on the positive qualities that make us unique, but I know you have the courage to do it with me. In the upcoming pages, I'll share some of my own super powers as a way to model what your exploration might look like.

If you don't explore your life story, wiring, and strengths, you'll be missing out on leveraging your super powers to carry out your unique vision. It's like wanting to travel to the other side of the globe but being afraid to fly. Your ability to *fly* (through the strength of your super powers) will allow you to go to places that you've been dreaming of. I'm not talking about physically traveling overseas (although that might be part of your vision). I'm talking about the power to propel your life to a whole new level by seeing your dreams and visions come to fruition.

3. Cultivate your super powers through intentional action.
Once you know what your super powers are, you have the opportunity to exercise them with intention. Rather than trying to do *everything* when it comes to carrying out your unique vision, choose your focus based on where you're strong and find other people who can fill in the gaps where they have their own super powers.

The 80/20 rule seems to apply here, doesn't it? Eighty percent of your effectiveness most likely comes from 20% of your effort. Once you realize what super powers are fueling that 20%, you can start to focus more intentionally in those areas.

My guess is that you have a sense of what your super powers are, but I want to take time to walk through the three main areas where they will be revealed. I can feel you getting fired up! Are you ready?

Your Life Story
Each of us has a story that's strung together by the highs, lows, and ordinary days of our lives. Some of us are younger, and our stories are rather short. Others of us are more mature, and there are more years behind us than in front of us. No matter what…your story *is* your story. It is no more or less important than the journey anyone else has taken.

Although our stories include the ordinary times of life, our narrative is most defined by the highs and lows we experience along the way. If you think back on your life, most of what you will remember will be those times when you experienced something extremely exhilarating or profoundly painful. These seasons (however long or short) compel you to define your story.

It's interesting to note that two different people can go through a similar situation, but the story they tell themselves is quite different. Two friends may go through a layoff at a large corporation. One takes on the role of a martyr, while the other sees it as an opportunity.

Two people…two different stories.

Although you may not be able to change the experiences you've walked through or the choices you've made, you *can* choose to see things from a different perspective. Most of these re-frames are possible as we look back on the painful experiences of life. It's not dismissing the pain, but it's seeing the events from a different angle, which will allow you to use your story as a super power.

What you've walked through in the past can be a super power to propel you into your future!

1. **Take time to reflect on the journey of your life.**
   Allow your mind's eye to travel back in time. Journey toward your earliest memories. Are they of your mom and dad, siblings, or someone else? What were you doing? Can you see what you were wearing?

Now…grow a little older in your mind. Do you remember special days as a kid? Days of playing outside with your brother or sister or friends? What games did you play? What did you talk about? Was there innocence to it all?

As you matured, can you remember times of adventure? How about beauty? When did you feel peaceful and at ease? Can you close your eyes and see moments full of love? How about when you first felt the transcendent presence of the Divine?

If you're having a hard time remembering your past, maybe you'll find it helpful to pull out an old photo album or scroll through some images on your computer. Maybe you'd like to flip through a high school yearbook or read through an old journal. Find an open door to your mind's eye and the depths of your heart that will allow you access to these precious memories of years gone by.

2. Remember when you felt most alive.

Now that you've taken a meandering journey through the past, I want to ask you to focus in on times when you felt most energized. It doesn't matter how old or young you were. Just allow your heart to lead you to a specific moment or season of life when you were thriving in some way.

Although most of us envision thriving in the form of external success (getting A's in school, graduating from college, or getting a new job), perhaps the thriving was more internal. Maybe, it wasn't a time in your life when you were *outwardly* thriving. Maybe you were thriving in the face of adversity.

What did it feel like? Do you remember adrenaline pumping through your veins? Or, was there an aura of peacefulness? Perhaps you were energetic and vigorous. As you see yourself in the past, were you smiling, laughing, and playing? Were you alone or with a large group? What did your body language say about your experience of the moment?

3. Remember when you felt most empty.

I know it may not be much fun, but I'd like to challenge you to do the same thing when life felt barren or hollow. To feel empty means that there was something lacking.

Think about a time when you were not only lacking something outwardly...but inwardly.

When was a time when you lacked peace? A time when you felt so stressed or anxious or burdened down. How about a season when you were without close friends or family who would stand with you? Sure, they may have been physically present, but maybe you felt alone and without community.

How about a job where you didn't feel like your gifts, talents, and passions were being fully utilized? What about a situation among a group of people where your thoughts or feelings weren't valued? You'll never forget those times, will you? They serve a purpose if you'll allow them to.

Now that you've reflected on the highs and lows of your life, I want to invite you to allow your story to highlight your real life super powers.

When you felt most alive, what super powers were you using? Don't skip over this question and keep reading. Take a moment and pause to reflect.

My mind immediately goes toward big goals and projects that required me to be stretched in my leadership skills, tenacity, and faith. I think of starting a church with a dozen people when I was 30 years old, producing and directing my first documentary with no experience, and putting on numerous large events over the years.

When I think of these experiences, I recognize that my real-life super powers include casting vision to a group of people, motivating others toward a meaningful goal, seeing a detailed road map to accomplish something, being resourceful with a small budget, and developing a confidence in my ability to pull off big things. Your super powers will be different, and they should be. Each of us are unique!

Now, as you think about those seasons of life when you felt most empty...the low points of life...what super powers were developed or strengthened during those times? Many super powers are forged in darkness, and we don't recognize them until later on in the light. Once again...pause and reflect.

As I think about my own journey, my mind immediately travels back in time to moving from Kentucky to California at age 16 as I left behind a lifetime of friends and had to learn to start over again. I'm reminded of being let go from a couple of jobs, which required me to look at my shortcomings and pick myself back up. And, the lowest of the low came at the point of burnout as I've shared earlier.

When I think of these challenging and painful experiences, I see real-life super powers being refined under intense heat and some painful pounding. Sometimes, the low points of life are brought on by the choices of others, but other times, we ourselves have made immature, poor, or reckless choices resulting in pain and hardship. Nevertheless, it's an opportunity for us to look back and see our super powers being formed.

As I look at these low points in my life, I recognize that I have the super power of starting over and getting back up again. I have the super power of looking at my shortcomings and taking ownership of where I have made a poor choice or decision. And, I have deep compassion for those who have hit bottom and are trying to start over themselves.

In the same way that I've stated my super powers, I want to encourage you to write yours down in the margins or the back of this book. Writing them down is a way of owning them, and at that point, you can intentionally lean into them as you move forward and live out your vision.

Your Wiring

Not only do we each have unique life stories, but we also have a particular wiring or personality. The way you are wired is a combination of qualities that make you uniquely you. While strengths tend to be geared toward certain outward activities, your wiring is the internal realm that determines how you approach the world around you. There are numerous personality profiles that can help you learn more about how you're wired from the inside out. Here are four popular ones...

Enneagram - a typology of nine interconnected personality types.

Myers Briggs Type Indicator - 16 distinct personality types.

DISC - four dimensions of Dominance, Influence, Steadiness, and Conscientiousness.

Personality Plus - four types including Choleric, Melancholy, Sanguine, and Phlegmatic.

None of the personalities revealed in these profiles should be seen as right, wrong, good, or bad. It must be understood that there are upsides and downsides to all of them. The purpose of the process is to observe and identify…not to judge or pigeonhole you into only functioning in one particular way. Remember that we are fluid human beings who can choose many different methods of interaction, but we do have a certain *wiring* that is most prominent.

Currently, there is a strong buzz around the Enneagram, which is the most complex of the four personality profiles. Because its origin is disputed, there isn't one particular test associated with this methodology. Instead, there are numerous books available that elaborate on the nine archetypes (numbered one through nine), which each have certain characteristics. Each archetype has *disintegration* and *integration* points, which are the types connected by the lines of the enneagram figure and are believed by some to influence a person in more adverse or relaxed circumstances. Have I confused you yet? (Google a free Enneagram test and learn more about yourself. I'm a One!)

Second in popularity would be the Myers Briggs Type Indicator, which denotes 16 distinctive personality types that result from the interactions among preferences. There is an official test available at www.myersbriggs. org and free off-brand versions around the web as well. I am an INTJ described as…"Have original minds and great drive for implementing their ideas and achieving their goals. Quickly see patterns in external events and develop long-range explanatory perspectives. When committed, organize a job and carry it through. Skeptical and independent, have high standards of competence and performance - for themselves and others."[22] Once again, dive in by taking the test online and inviting your friends and family to take it as well.

Both the DISC (www.discprofile.com) and Personality Plus (www.classervices.com) profiles are easier to assimilate, but less robust in their depth. Although both are administered through a series of questions, perhaps you can pick out which Personality Plus profile most resembles your wiring through a simple overview.

If you are a *Choleric*, you're usually focused on getting things done and can accidentally run over people in the process. You can be both decisive and stubborn. Cholerics are leaders who are passionate about their vision.

A *Melancholy* is a highly talented person who develops brilliant ideas. They can often paralyze themselves with over-analysis. If you are a Melancholy, you are passionate about lists and doing things the *right* way.

If you are a *Sanguine*, you get along well with people and can get others excited about your interests. Unfortunately, you can't always be relied upon to get things done...especially the details. You love being with others and play the role of the entertainer in group interactions. You may have a tendency to over-promise and under-deliver.

Finally, a *Phlegmatic* is stable and most neutral. Although you may not actively upset people, your indifference may frustrate those around you. You are comfortable not making decisions and generally fine with the status quo. You care about the harmony of the people around you.

A simplification might be that a Choleric likes it *my* way, a Melancholy likes it the *right* way, a Sanguine likes it the *fun* way, and a Phlegmatic likes it the *easy* way. The truth is that you are wired uniquely and beautifully, and your wiring is part of the foundation of your identity.

No matter which personality profile you utilize (Enneagram, Myers Briggs, DISC, or Personality Plus), you will be able to learn more about the super powers found within your wiring. Each one of these profiles has helped me learn more about myself and celebrate my one-of-a-kind personality.

I will tell you that I have struggled with the downsides of my personality over the years. I am driven, visionary, focused, goal-oriented, and passionate, which also means that I can overwork, lose sight of relationships, believe I know the right way of doing something, and communicate in ways that are too intense...just to name a few.

I have incredible super powers that are revealed in my wiring, and I have also come to embrace that I have some downsides. I've spent the last 25 years working to minimize those downsides through character formation and skill development, but they will always be a challenge for me. When I inadvertently hurt someone because of the downsides of my super powers, I take ownership, apologize, seek to repair, and move forward. I say all of that, because I want you to be intensely confident in your super powers and equally as humble in the downsides that come along with them.

Your Strengths

You're starting to understand your unique wiring or the internal realm that determines how you approach the world around you, but now I want you to take a look at your strengths, a natural propensity toward certain activities (also known as talents). You have a combination of strong points that only you possess. No one else is exactly like you. If you have brothers or sisters, it was very clear to you during your growing up years that they were stronger than you in certain ways.

Perhaps, you were disappointed by the fact that they excelled in sports while you struggled...or they got good grades while you had to study extra hard. On the other hand, you may have gloated (just a bit) when it became apparent that you were able to outperform them in some other activity.

From an early age, my wife and I have seen the uniqueness of strengths play out in our own children. Emerson has always been quite adept at navigating his way around any sort of technology. On the other hand, Waverly is intensely passionate about fashion. We don't try to make Emerson be just like Waverly or vice versa. We highlight the strengths of each of them and cheer them on...knowing that they are both unique human beings.

Think about your own strengths for a moment. What do you have a natural disposition toward? Are you gifted in using your hands to create or fix things? Do you cook and serve those around you with grace and ease? Or, maybe you are passionate about numbers and they just come easy for you.

You were created with gifts, talents, and inclinations that can be nurtured and developed even further. There's very little sense in focusing on your weaknesses and trying to turn those into strengths. I've never seen anyone do that. Sure, you'd be wise to minimize those weaknesses as I mentioned earlier, but your real focus should be on those areas where you're uniquely gifted.

The most helpful tool on the market to discover your strengths is called *CliftonStrengths* (formerly known as *StrengthsFinder*), which can be found at www.gallup.com/cliftonstrengths. Created by Don Clifton and now published by Gallup, the CliftonStrengths assessment can help you uncover your unique combination of 34 CliftonStrengths themes. It is a paid test that is well worth taking if you're serious about understanding your real-life super powers. For example, my top five CliftonStrengths themes are...

Futuristic - inspired by the future and what could be. They energize others with their visions of the future.

Activator - can make things happen by turning thoughts into action. They want to do things now, rather than simply talk about them.

Command - has a strong presence. They can take control of a situation and make decisions.

Competition - measure their progress against the performance of others. They strive to win first place and revel in contests.

Input - have a need to collect and archive. They may accumulate information, ideas, artifacts or even relationships.

When I first saw these results, I felt deeply known as a human being. It felt so good for someone (okay, it was actually just a computer) to know me so deeply. I've been able to leverage these five strengths as my super powers over and over again when it comes to my life and leadership. Take the real assessment - not a knock-off that you Google online. It's worth it.

Beyond this online tool, you'd be well served to start asking people who are close to you. Tell them that you're trying to discover your strengths so that you can maximize them and build upon them. A true friend will be happy to encourage you in this way. By focusing on the places in your life where you're already strong, don't be surprised when you increase your effectiveness double, quadruple, or even a hundredfold.

Cultivating Your Super Powers

Now that you're starting to identify your real-life super powers, it's time to cultivate them through intentional action. As you're going about your daily life, I want to encourage you to notice when things are quick or easy for you...moments when you feel like you're in the flow...when time just seems to fly by without you noticing...or when you feel full of energy and life.

In those moments, ask yourself, "What super powers am I using right now?" My guess is you'll start to notice the same super powers coming up over and over again. You'll also want to be aware when something feels like drudgery...like it will never end. In these moments, you're obviously not using your super powers, and I would encourage you to ask two questions...

1. Is it possible for me to use my super powers to do this task?
You may be trying to complete the task by doing it how *other* people have suggested. What if you looked at the task through the lens of your life story, wiring, and strengths? Is there another way to get it done? Just because your parents or partner or co-workers do something a certain way, it doesn't mean that *you* can't go about it in a way that's more in alignment with your own super powers.

2. Is it possible for someone else to do the task?
I'm a big fan of spending money to decrease my pain and increase my time. That's why I pay someone else to do my bookkeeping and taxes - both tasks that I absolutely abhor. Think about things you're doing right now that could be done by someone else for free, trade, or payment. It could be anything from mowing your lawn to cleaning your home to organizing your garage. The list of what you can have other people do when it isn't one of your super powers is endless.

My goal for you is to utilize your super powers more often so that you're in the *flow* each and every day. You know why? Because the world needs what's within you. Your family, friends, and community desperately need your unique vision to come to fruition, and they need you to be using your super powers in the process.

Say it with me. *My life story, wiring, and strengths are my super powers.*

Chapter 6

I HAVE A HEART FOR OTHERS

"I am learning to use them with others - for the sake of others."

I have a deep love for Circle K. Oh, you've never been to one? Imagine a convenience store that's a notch below 7-Eleven with less expensive fountain drinks and a huge selection of alcohol and lottery tickets. Of those three, I opt for the fountain drink on an almost daily basis.

Why do I get my Diet Dr. Pepper at Circle K when I could just go to a grocery store? Frankly, I love the experience. I like the ritual of going inside, taking a deep breath, saying 'hi' to the cashiers, dispensing the crunchy ice, and hearing the gushing sound of the glorious DDP filling my extra-large cup.

I know it's weird, but it's okay. I am inspired. I am enough. I am loved.

One day I strike up a conversation with Maria, a cashier who I see often, and I learn that she has a son and daughter. A few days later, I see her and her kids shopping at Home Depot, and I get to meet them both. Each time I stop by Circle K, her face lights up, and we exchange a bit of small talk.

With the holidays approaching, I ask her if Circle K will be open on Christmas day, and she says they never close. In fact, she tells me that she'll be working on Christmas day herself! Through a back and forth conversation, I learn that her brother (and others in the home) watch her kids while she works 40+ hours a week.

"Are you married?" I ask...noticing the ring on her finger.

"Oh, yes, but my husband had to go to Mexico about five months ago."

"Was he deported?"

She goes on to tell me about the trouble he encountered with his attorney who didn't file the right paperwork for his green card renewal.

"When did he come to the States?"

"1980...when he was seven years old," she says. "With his older brother."

That means her husband is 47 years old...the same age as me.

I learn that Maria moved here in 2000, and she has worked at the same Circle K for 15 years. (Let that sink in for a moment.) Meanwhile, her husband is living outside of Mexico City and raising crops and animals to get by.

Questions flood my mind like...why didn't her husband pursue citizenship? Did he seek help? What level of education does he have? Who could have helped him? Why didn't he help himself? What's the story with his attorney? Is this a systemic issue? The truth is that I have no answers...but I know I have friends across the political spectrum with strong opinions about immigration.

Want to know the main question that opened up all this conversation? I simply asked, "What are you getting your kids for Christmas?"

"I'm not sure what I can get them. You know how kids always want so much," she responds.

"What do they want?" I ask.

"I haven't opened up their letters to Santa yet, but I know my son wants some goalie gloves and a soccer ball. Not much I guess."

As tears welled up in her eyes, she said, "I'm sorry for telling you all this stuff."

We part ways, but I can't stop thinking about Maria and her kids. I know our family can help in a small way, but I feel like I want to do more.

I simply post the story on Facebook and write, "Our family is going to buy a couple of gift cards - one to Target and one to Big 5 Sporting Goods - so that Maria can have extra resources to shop for her kids this Christmas. If you want to add to the amount, you can DM me."

Within 24 hours, numerous friends chipped in, and we amassed a total of $650!

The next day, I return to the store and tell Maria that I had shared her story with a few of my friends. I hand her a Christmas card with a $50 gift card from Big 5 Sporting Goods so she could buy her son a soccer ball and goalie gloves.

Tears begin to well up in her eyes, and her heart gushes with thankfulness.

Then, I pull out a $500 gift card from Target so she can treat her family to an amazing Christmas. At this point, she is overwhelmed and speechless.

Then, I tell her that my friends thought she might spend all the money on her kids, so we should get something just for her. I pull out a $100 gift card from Target and tell her she can only spend it on herself!

At that point, Maria tells me that one of my friends stopped by earlier in the day and gave her a hundred dollar bill. WOW!

Maria tells me, "God surprises me every day! I've never had a Christmas like this."

Do For One
In these moments, I wish I had the resources to help the entire world, but I'm just one person. The reality is that there are unending needs that can't be met by any one person or church or organization or country.

Everyone can play a role in helping others.

I also realize that our gift to Maria was simply relief from the systemic challenges that she faces every day. Other people are working on those *big* issues, but I know Maria. She rings up my Diet Dr. Pepper, and I now know her kids.

Andy Stanley says, "Do for one what you wish you could do for everyone. Because if we all did for one what we wish we could do for everyone, it might change the world. But certainly, it would change one person's world. It may even change your world."[23]

There are so many reasons why I don't help other people more often. There's a voice yelling in my head, "I don't have enough time or money. I don't know where to start. I don't think it will make a difference. It's not my problem." But, here's the reality...

1. **We're all connected in this world.**
   In our North American self-sufficient culture, it's easy to think that we live autonomous lives that are disconnected from the problems and challenges of others. In my faith tradition, it is said, "When one suffers, we all suffer."[24] When someone in your community passes away, there is a sense of loss among those who were connected. From a societal perspective, when someone is experiencing homelessness or severe illness without insurance, the economic impact on our world is serious.

   Martin Luther King writes, "Injustice anywhere is a threat to justice everywhere. We are caught in an inescapable network of mutuality, tied in a single garment of destiny. Whatever affects one directly, affects all indirectly."[25]

   When you help someone, you're helping us all. Thank you for investing in a healthy relationship with your partner and children. Thank you for giving to organizations that are doing good in the world. Thank you for being kind to the person who is having a tough day. When you help them, you're helping me, and I appreciate it.

2. **When we help others, we cultivate generosity and love.**
   Do you think our world would be a better place with more generosity and more love? I believe that wholeheartedly, and that's why you and I have the opportunity to plant seeds wherever we go.

   When you open the door for someone you don't know...
   When you pay for another's coffee...
   When you take time to listen...
   When you take a meal to someone in need...
   When you give generously to organizations who are doing good...
   When you see a need on Facebook and you respond...
   you are planting seeds of generosity and love that will spring up in the lives of other people.

From the people you help...to the people who saw you help...to your own family and friends, people will be inspired by your generosity and love, and they will pass it along in time. It may not return to you personally, but it will be passed along to others. We desperately need that in our world.

3. We invest our time and money in things that matter to us.
Yes, I know you're busy, and I know you have lots of bills. Yet, you are in control of how you spend both your time and money. You choose how long you lay in bed, what you do during your commute, how you spend your lunch break, what activities you enroll your children in, and how you spend your free time. At one point or another, you choose how you invest your time.

The same is true about money. In your current situation, you have access to a certain amount of financial resources, and you choose how you spend it. You choose where you live, what car you drive, the food you eat, the clothes you wear, the phone you use, and the entertainment you consume.

I'm not saying that *how* you invest your time or money is right, wrong, good, or bad, but just want you (and me) to fully realize that we have been empowered to make choices. You are making choices regarding your time and money based on what you value... what matters most to you in the moment.

And, here's the wacky thing that is true as well...*where* you invest your time and money is *where* you'll cultivate meaning and love. In other words, if you want to care more about a person or issue in this world, give your time and money. All of a sudden, you'll start feeling a deeper care and love for that person or situation because you're invested. Try it.

For the Sake of Others

As you allow your unique vision to flow from your heart, I want to invite you to ask yourself, "How is my vision *for* the sake of others?" Your vision is flowing from an interest or passion within *you*. There's a joy present when you think about whatever it is that you're dreaming of, and that feels good.

Julie Parker, founder of The Beautiful You Coaching Academy, asks us, "How will you serve the world? How through serving yourself will you serve your sisters and brothers and children around you? How will you serve your community? How will you show up online in a way that truly makes a difference to us all?"[26]

Now might be a good time to re-visit the Inspiration Rising Manifesto. Although we've been diving in to each sentence along the way, I want us to read the entire thing once again to see the context of using our super powers for the sake of others.

Will you read it out loud with me?

Inspiration Rising Manifesto

My life has been inspired from the moment of conception.
I am whole and complete just as I am.
I don't have to do or be anything else to be loved.

This is my true identity.

Embracing my inspired-ness, I am discovering my
unique way to bring inspiration to the world.
My life story, wiring, and strengths are my super powers,
and I am learning to use them with others
- for the sake of others.

I have access to all the resources I need to live out my inspiration,
and I will be strong and courageous in the face of any challenge.

My inspiration is rising.

I believe that part of the reason we are here on this planet is to help other people. Have you ever been to a memorial service for someone who was known to be self-centered, greedy, and consumed by accomplishments, work, and physical possessions? I have. In fact, I've officiated a couple of funerals for people like that, and the open mic time is brutal. People tell funny stories, but they aren't very heartfelt. It's hollow, and I know that's not the kind of legacy you want to leave.

I HAVE A HEART FOR OTHERS

As you embrace your true identity, you'll discover a unique vision within your heart, and our world desperately needs what you have to offer. As you've learned, you have super powers, and I'm challenging you to use them *for* the sake of others. These super powers have not been given to you and cultivated by you simply for your own benefit.

Yes, you will benefit. You will feel good as you work toward making your vision come to fruition. You will benefit relationally, because people will want to be around your positive energy. You will benefit mentally as your mind is stretched by new opportunities and challenges. You will benefit financially as you are rewarded for the value you bring to the world.

At the same time, how will your vision bring benefit to the people around you...and even the world at large?

Jacqui, who you met in chapter four, has a vision of a flower farm as you re-member. Imagine if she bought the 6.5-acre property, renovated the house, planted acres of flowers, and simply enjoyed them for herself. She could walk through the fields and take selfies among the beautiful blooms, and her home would be filled with the fragrance of an abundance of bouquets. But, no one else would ever enjoy them.

That would be kinda weird, huh?
That's because a vision without benefit to others is a *hollow* vision.

Instead, she envisions bringing beauty into the homes and offices of people throughout the Portland area, she imagines flower essential oils diffusing in the air, and she dreams of a flower festival where families come to enjoy the farm.

Her vision may be focused on flowers, but it's infused with beauty, health, and relationships...*for* the sake of others.

How does your unique vision bring benefit to...
your family,
your friends,
your community,
a unique niche,
or the world at large?

I have found that people who are motivated by a vision that benefits others in some way (large or small) are more likely to succeed at whatever they are seeking to accomplish. It's not just about you or me. It's about bringing something of value to people who need what you have to offer.

Using Your Super Powers *With* Others

I grew up as an only child. Just me and my parents, and I got all the attention in the world. I wouldn't go so far to say that I was spoiled, but I definitely wasn't forced to share much of anything. That is, until my parents chose to foster a girl from Guatemala who was in the United States for treatment of a hearing issue.

When she moved into our home during my junior high years, I was less than hospitable. All of a sudden, my dad was doting on this new kid, and my mom was figuring out what to cook that she would enjoy.

"What about me?!?!?!" I thought.

I took out my feelings of resentment toward her through sneers and rolling my eyes and ignoring this intruder in my home.

Several years later when we moved from Kentucky to California, my parents felt like it was best for her to transition into another foster family, and I wasn't sad about it. (Geez, what a jerk I was!)

Years later during college, I watched a 20/20 television special about the organization that brought the girl to the U.S. for her surgeries, and I saw her in the background on television. My heart sank with sadness at how I had treated her, and I reached out to that organization, which informed me that she had moved back to Guatemala.

I was just a gangly teenager trying to find my way, but I was overly insecure about my place in the world. I didn't have the skills to be *with* another kid in my home. Part of that was growing up as an only child, and part was simply my personality.

To this day, I am a slight introvert, and I often prefer doing something on my own or by myself rather than needing to involve someone else...especially when it comes to a work project. Oftentimes, I think I can do it faster or better than if someone else was involved.

I HAVE A HEART FOR OTHERS

Working with others has never been my strong suit, and that's why I included it in the Inspiration Rising Manifesto. If you read that line "with others" and that's a no-brainer for you, just know that those two words are for me personally. I need them.

Everyday when I read the manifesto, I want to be reminded that I actually need to work with others, and here's why...

1. Other people are strong where I'm weak.
Patience and sensitivity with others, networking at parties, driving safely, and manly outdoor skills are just a few areas of my life where I am most certainly weak. Thank God for my wife who is strong in all those areas!

If we're navigating a sensitive issue with our kids...
If we're going to a party where I don't know people...
If we're driving anywhere...
If we need to grill or cut or mow something...
my wife is taking the lead for sure.

When I take the time to invite others to be *with* me in whatever I'm doing, I find that I always learn something new. They have super powers...their life story, wiring, and strengths...that I don't have, and I'm better off being around them.

2. Other people can see things I can't see.
Because of my own life story, wiring, and strengths, I'm blind to the experiences and challenges of others. In reality, I haven't walked in their shoes. The beauty of involving others in your vision is that you'll have the opportunity to see things from another person's perspective (if you allow them to speak into it).

This is one of the reasons why I love interviewing female leaders and entrepreneurs on the Inspiration Rising podcast. I have so much to learn from each and every guest, and I willingly ask the most ignorant questions. Even though I prepare for every interview, I will undoubtedly ask something that may seem simple to the interviewee, but it's new information to me.

When I'm willing to humble myself and ask questions that I don't know the answers to, I am positioning myself as a lifelong learner.

I have something to learn from every person on the planet, be-cause they can see things I can't see.

3. **Other people need me, and I need them.**

While it may be easier to do something on my own, there are peo-ple that need me to help them in some way. They may need to be taught, mentored, challenged, or encouraged, and the only way that can happen is if I am connected and doing things *with* others. And, the same is true for me. I need other people even if I don't think I do. In my most mentally and emotionally sober moments... usually when something isn't going so great in my life...I can fully admit my need for others.

I need other people to...
teach me what they know,
share their experiences with me,
challenge me on my thinking,
encourage me when I'm down,
and walk with me as companions on the journey of life.

What would it look like to invite others to walk with you as you bring your inspiration to the world?

Sending Maria and Her Kids Off

Because Maria's husband was deported to Mexico, she and the kids had not seen him for months. With no money to hire an immigration attorney, they felt like the best option was to move and be a reunited family. The kids were excited to see their dad, but Maria knew life was going to be differ-ent...and difficult.

During one visit to Circle K, I see Maria's eyes well up with tears as she tells me they are moving to be with her husband. After saving up enough mon-ey, they bought bus tickets and scheduled their departure.

Maria invites my wife and I over to the apartment she shares with her brother's family in order to pray for her and the kids before they leave.

When my wife and I walk in, we immediately notice sheets hanging from the ceiling in order to create a privacy curtain along the small living room. A mattress is positioned where a couch would be, and I realize this had been their family's room.

I HAVE A HEART FOR OTHERS

We walk down the makeshift hallway into the kitchen where Maria's kids are waiting for us. We talk about their excitement for the bus ride and the snacks they have ready for the journey. My wife, who speaks Spanish, is able to speak with Maria to a depth that I have not been able. Her son shares a giant pad of artwork and a painted canvas with us, and he asks me to keep it for him while they are gone.

We huddle around them and pray for safety and provision as they step into a new reality. I hand her some money as a token of my care for her family even though I was just getting to know them.

I don't know how much we helped them, but we did what we could with the resources we had. I didn't do it alone. I did it with others - for the sake of others, and you can, too.

Section 3

BRINGING YOUR INSPIRATION
TO THE WORLD

Chapter 7
I WILL TAKE ACTION
"I have access to all the resources I need to live out my inspiration."

Have you ever found yourself in a situation where quick, decisive action was needed? Something was happening, and someone needed to jump in and do something right away!

- A house on fire with people asleep inside?
- A car accident where people need medical attention?
- A swimmer caught in an ocean riptide and can't get out?
- A motorist breaks down and needs a push?
- A lost child in the middle of a giant store?
- A loose dog running in the street?

There's one thing in common with all these situations.
There is an *urgent need*!

Someone or something is in need of assistance. Sure, maybe they could manage on their own, but I don't want to take the chance that they'll make it out alive. Beyond the physical danger of the moment, there's the possibility of emotional trauma of being involved in a situation that's scary and maybe even life-threatening.

In those moments when I've stayed with a driver after a crash, gotten the attention of a lifeguard, pushed a car out of the road, helped a lost child toward security, or reunited a dog with its owner, that person shows deep gratitude for the action I've taken. It's not just about the physical support, but also the emotional.

Not only is there a *need* in each of these situations, but there is a sense of *urgency*. The *need* calls upon our compassion, but the *urgency* compels us to react right away.

If we only see a need, many of us simply end up feeling overwhelmed or even depressed. If you hear that a dog shelter has 50 dogs that need to be adopted, you may think to yourself, "I hope someone helps those dogs." If you hear that the same shelter has lost funding and is planning to euthanize all 50 dogs at the end of the week, you're more likely to say, "We need to find homes for those dogs. Who do we know that wants one?"

Do you see the difference? A need can evoke emotion, but a need *plus* a sense of urgency motivates action.

On the other hand, have you ever experienced someone try to create urgency without a real need? This is the friend or family member who runs around yelling, "The sky is falling! The sky is falling!" They're freaking out about their life or work, but you have a sense that they're overstating the level of the situation. Urgency without need creates suspicion and even mistrust.

If you're going to see your unique vision come to fruition...
If you're going to have the relationships you desire...
If you're going to experience better physical health...
If you're going to grow in your spirituality...
If you're going to start that side hustle or get that new job...
If you're going to increase your finances...
you must see the need *and* create a sense of urgency.

What's Holding You Back?
There's something you want to do in your life. Before you picked up this book, there was something swirling in your head and heart that you want to do, finish, or experience in the next six to twelve months, and I'm here to help you make that happen!

My question is...Why haven't you taken action up until now? What's holding you back? What's preventing you from starting, pushing through the middle, and finishing whatever it is you desire? As I work with women (and men) on a daily basis, I find there are three main things holding people back. See if you resonate with one or more.

1. Negative Thinking
When you think about your unique vision (whatever it is), you hear voices inside your head that spew negative thoughts.

"You don't deserve _____."
"You're not _____ enough."

"You've failed in the past. Why even try?"
"People won't support you."
"People will laugh at you."

In those moments when you're paralyzed, procrastinating, or putting something off, ask yourself, "What am I hearing that is preventing me from taking action?" My guess is that you'll find some negative thinking that's holding you back. Turn back to chapter three and dive into your divine imprint. Re-read those 20 statements inserting your name to interrupt this stinkin' thinkin' and embrace your true identity.

2. Negative Life Experiences

We've all had challenging and painful experiences in life, haven't we? Unfortunately, many of us make a vow in the midst of that experience that prevents us from pushing through a similar situation when it comes up in the future.

A vow may sound like...
"I'll never trust someone like that ever again."
"I'll never work with a partner ever again."
"I'll never invest that kind of money ever again."

If you've ever said something like this, you're not alone. In the midst of pain and disappointment, I've said plenty of things like this. When we make these kind of vows, we're taking a single person or situation and making a blanket judgment for the rest of our lives. We're limiting ourselves from experiencing something that may be needed in order for us to fulfill the vision in our hearts.

What if we saw these life experiences through the lens of learning? Instead of making a vow laced with pain and disappointment, what if we asked, "What can I learn from this person or experience without assuming all people or experiences will be like this?"

3. Negative People in Your Life

Who have you allowed to pull a seat up to the table of your life and speak negativity into your ears? Maybe it's a family member that you feel like you just can't get away from....or a long-time friend who always sees the glass as half-empty...or a co-worker who complains about your boss or workload or customers or all three.

I know what it's like to feel stuck in a negative or one-sided relationship, and I also know what it's like to finally muster up the courage to say something. In these moments, you and I can redirect the conversation to something more positive, ask the person to stop putting you or others down, express a desire to be more positive in your life, set a boundary when the person continues to spread negativity, or even transition out of the friendship.

Earlier in my life, I had a very close friend who seemed to find great pleasure in poking at my insecurities. Over the years, his verbal jabs added up, and my efforts to blow them off or express my discomfort didn't work. When I started to withdraw from the friendship, he obviously noticed, and we had a difficult conversation. He was unwilling to modify his communication style and thought I should toughen up. I set a clear boundary and chose to walk away from the friendship. I instantly felt a relief.

If you're putting up with negativity, harassment, or lack of support, you are allowing someone to hold you back from being the best version of yourself. Sure, you want people who can speak truth in moments when you're really blowing it, but those times are few and far between. You need people who will believe the best about you, support you in your dreams, and encourage you every step of the way...even when you fall.

Turning a Setback into a Comeback

Having been recruited by the business owners, Rhonda was elated at the opportunity to help a new beauty clinic get off the ground. (Think laser hair removal, microblading, Botox, and the like.) While the owners focused on acquiring the location, purchasing the equipment, and getting certified on the procedures, Rhonda was responsible for developing standard operating procedures, marketing, and customer service. She was getting rave reviews and was even invited along on a business trip to Paris![27]

After employees were hired and the doors were opened, the business began to soar, but Rhonda was let go with no notice at all. No write-ups. No complaints. No warning.

Imagine the feeling of pouring your heart and soul into a business and being let go after you put all the systems in place. She was heartbroken to say the least. She felt used and betrayed, but she had no recourse.

Rhonda's confidence was at rock bottom, and she knew she needed help to get unstuck. When she started the Launch Your Life coaching program, her pain spilled over into tears during our mastermind video calls. It was clear that this negative experience could cripple her if she didn't experience a breakthrough.

Week after week, Rhonda started to embrace her true identity as she learned about her divine imprint, looked back at her life story, and dug into her wiring and strengths. Meanwhile, her fellow group members would cheer her on during our weekly calls to encourage her to keep moving forward.

As the group experienced several visualizations designed to allow them to uncover a vision for the next season of their lives, Rhonda saw a mental picture of her preferable future. She saw herself working from home in front of two large computer monitors as she helped an array of beauty clinics across the country with their social media marketing. This would allow her to leverage her industry experience empowered by her administrative and marketing skills.

With this vision locked in her mind and heart, Rhonda and I worked together to help her set tangible goals and accompanying action steps within a workable timetable. Within a matter of weeks, she decided on a company name, built a website, and started connecting with potential clients.[28] By embracing her true identity and uncovering her super powers, she could finally bring her inspiration to the world.

Lock In Your Vision and Feel It
My hope is that you've started to allow a vision to cultivate in your heart and mind. It can truly be anything that you deeply desire. From getting healthy to starting a side hustle to finding a life partner, you're the one who knows what your heart desires. Now is the time to lock it in and feel it.

As we've learned, your vision is a mental picture of your preferable future. It's a snapshot in time that embodied what you desire. No, it doesn't show all of the details, but it's a moment that represents the end result that you want in your life.

For example, when I produced and directed a documentary on sex trafficking in the United States, I envisioned 100 theaters across America full of people absolutely gripped by the stories of the survivors and the female abolitionists who helped them.[29] In the midst of all the trips to film the stories, the editing, the sound design, the color correction, and everything else that goes along with indie filmmaking, I kept this vision in my mind's eye. This mental picture is what allowed me to push through the messy middle when all I wanted to do was quit.

For me, this vision was fueled by an *urgent need*. While thousands of women and children are sold for sex every day in the United States, many people are oblivious to what's happening in their own towns and cities. In my mind, people *needed* to be educated on this subject. Women and children *needed* to be rescued and rehabilitated. Schools and communities *needed* to do something to prevent this from happening to others.

Not only was there a need, but I sensed an *urgency* for two reasons. First of all, this is an issue that impacts all our communities, and the lives of women and children are at stake. I wanted to educate people as quickly as possible. Even though there were many other films and resources on the subject when I produced this in 2015, I had a personal urgency to reach more people and in a different way. I was under no delusion that my film and accompanying resources were the solution to education, but I knew I had a burning passion within me to take action.

The second source of urgency was self-imposed. Because of the breadth of the project, I knew it could drag on for a long time, and I had witnessed other documentary filmmakers take years to finish a film. I wanted to shoot, edit, and release the movie within one year, and this created an urgency to take action daily.

Guess what? That movie has been shown at over 350 grassroots screenings around the United States including universities, high schools, police departments, community centers, non-profits, and churches. In the process, thousands of people have been educated on the subject. In addition to the documentary, I produced a compilation benefit music album to raise money for one of the featured organizations, and I wrote and published three other books to help people engage the subject in different ways.

Not only has the film been used to raise thousands of dollars for organizations that are fighting to end sex trafficking, but there is one verified case where a young woman watched the film and realized that she was being trafficked herself. What was normal to her would be horrific to all of us, and as a result of watching the film, she was rescued and is on her journey of healing.

An urgent need was embedded in my vision, and the results have been tremendous!

What is your unique vision? It doesn't need to be starting a social media marketing company like Rhonda or producing a documentary like me. It could be absolutely anything that is welling up in your heart. See it through the lens of a *need*.

Even if your vision for the next six months is cleaning up your backyard and putting in landscaping. Don't just see it as a project that you've wanted to check off the list. See it as an opportunity to create a peaceful oasis where your family can relax and connect with friends. Your family *needs* this space for their mental and relational health. Do you feel the difference between seeing your vision as something you just want to check off your list...versus seeing the underlying need?

Now, how are you going to inject a sense of urgency into your vision? You can have a beautiful mental picture of your backyard that's been bottled up in your mind for years. If you don't create urgency around your vision, it probably won't ever come to fruition.

In a similar situation, I asked a client this question, "In the next six months, what are some important celebrations? Birthdays, graduations, anniversaries?"

She said, "Well, we have several birthdays in our family about three months from now."

"Great! Let's pick a Saturday to have a party in your backyard!"

"But...my backyard isn't ready yet," she protested.

"That's the point!" I said with a big smile on my face.

I introduced a sense of urgency in her vision that would motivate her and her family to take action. Guess what? It happened. She set the date, sent out e-vites, and she rallied her family to get the backyard in shape. It would never have happened without the sense of urgency.

Now, let's talk about you. From changing the state of your marriage to bettering your health to finishing your degree to taking a trip overseas...lock in a mental picture that embodies the moment in time when you know your vision has come to fruition.

Next, I want you to feel it. What will it feel like in that moment?

When producing my films, I envision myself standing on the side of the theatre as people are watching the big screen. In almost every screening of my four films, I stand off to the side and never sit down. I'm too excited for people to watch the movie, and I want to see their faces. I want to see when they laugh unexpectedly. I want to see what grips them. And, I want to see their eyes well up in tears during touching moments. When I see their emotions, it makes me feel something powerful. When I want to lock in my vision, I take a deep breath and feel all those amazing emotions and a profound sense of accomplishment.

When you close your eyes and allow your mind to create this powerful mental picture of your preferable future, what will you feel in that moment? Excitement, joy, power, strength, gratitude, exhilaration? Whatever it is, feel it right now as you lock in that vision. As you're going after the vision, this feeling will drive you even more.

All the Resources You Need
As your vision takes shape in your mind's eye, one of the things you may be thinking is, "I have no idea how I can possibly pull this off." You may be concerned about a lack of knowledge, experience, connections, time, or money, but I'm telling you that you have access to all the resources you need to live out your inspiration. Let me show you how...

- **You have access to knowledge.**
  "I don't know how to _____." Fill in the blank. I don't care what it is that you think you don't know, you can find the answer on the Internet. Someone has made a website, blog post, video, or online course about the subject. You have absolutely no excuse for a lack of knowledge, because you can go get it for *free* if you're willing to look.

  Here's a list of things that I've learned on my own by using the Internet - graphic design, web development, social media marketing, screen writing, photography and videography techniques, video editing, incorporating a business, selling on eBay/Amazon/Etsy/iTunes, podcast recording / editing, and manufacturing overseas.

This is just a small list of things that I've learned online, and over the years, I've generated income with every single one of these skills.

Beyond the Internet, you also have free access to local libraries and thousands of podcasts. If you want to spend a bit of money, you have access to unending knowledge through books on Amazon and audio books on Audible. If you want to learn something, you already have access. You just have to seek it out.

- **You have access to experience.**
  We all have a limited number of experiences to this point in our lives, but we have access to other people who have had different experiences than our own. If you want to know how to do something that goes beyond mere knowledge, seek out someone who has done it already.

Kelsey Chapman, author of *What They Taught Me: Extraordinary Life Lessons from Ordinary Women*, shared with me, "It seems like for every season I've needed someone to guide me. Someone's been there for that exact role. I've had someone step in for every season, and it's forever impacted my life. It's gotten me further than I could have ever gone alone. That's why I'm really passionate about mentoring."[30]

Ask them out to coffee, or contact them online if they're outside your area. If they're too busy or simply decline, move on and ask someone else. In the process, always be sure to offer your experience, support, or just a listening ear. You don't want this to be a mere transaction. You want a mutually-beneficial relationship where you genuinely care for them and their vision as well.

- **You have access to connections.**
  There's a strong possibility that you need the help of someone else in order to see your vision come to fruition, and you may not know that person already. After determining the person or type of people you'd like to know, what would it look like to ask a friend, family member, or colleague for an introduction? What about introducing yourself via email or social media? Reach out and be genuinely interested in them while being clear about your vision and how they might be able to help you.

- **You have access to time.**
  You choose how you spend every moment of your day. You choose when you wake up and when you go to bed. You choose how long it takes you to get ready in the morning and at night. You choose how you spend your work hours, lunch, and after hours. You choose. If you truly want to see your vision come to fruition, you will reallocate your time to be able to invest in your goals and action steps. Other people have the same 24 hours in their day, and they're able to go after their goals. If your vision was an urgent need, how would you change the way you spend your time?

- **You have access to money and physical resources.**
  No matter your socio-economic level, I guarantee that you have access to all the resources you need to live out your inspiration. You know how I know that? Because I've done it.

  I've literally gone to estate sales to buy stuff that dead people left behind in order to sell it for a profit on Craigslist, Facebook, and eBay in order to purchase a new camera. I've taken on side projects to pay for a family vacation. I've bartered my services with friends in order to get access to a physical location to shoot a video. I've raised money through a non-profit to fund three movies, and I sought out investors to fund another one.

  If you don't have the money, equipment, or physical location, you can get access to all those things if you're willing to be creative. Work a side job. Sell stuff you already own. Barter or trade. Ask for a donation. You may not be able to start a restaurant with the $100 you have in your checking account, but you can definitely host a pop-up dinner in your home or apartment. You can always start small and work toward expansion.

Setting Goals and Determining Action Steps

Now that you have your vision locked in and you're starting to feel it deeply, it's time to set goals that will bring this vision to fruition. Let's take the backyard transformation as an example. Because it's a relatively small project, I would set two primary goals. The first goal is the completion of the backyard transformation, and the second goal is the party itself. After setting these two goals with specific dates, I would create action steps under each goal. Here's an example...

Goal #1: Transform the backyard into a peaceful, hospitable space within four weeks.
  • Determine a spending limit.
  • Create an itemized budget.
  • Remove all unwanted items, weeds, and bushes.
  • Plant new flowers in pots.
  • And so on...

Goal #2: Host a backyard party for 25 friends five weeks from now.
  • Determine a spending limit.
  • Create an itemized budget.
  • Make an invite list and send e-vites.
  • Shop for food and drinks.
  • And so on...

If you felt the need to transform your backyard but didn't set a goal or create accompanying action steps along with deadlines, you'll probably never actually finish the project. For most people, if it doesn't end up on a list or a calendar, it probably won't get done.

If you want to experience something different in your life, you need to lock in your vision and feel it. You need to write down one or more goals that will help you experience that vision, and you'll need multiple action steps with deadlines in order to reach those goals. You're simply dreaming if you want to accomplish something in your life without taking these necessary steps.

Keep It In Front of You
My guess is that your vision isn't the only thing you have going on in your life. You probably have a job, family, friends, and all sorts of other things. For me, out of sight ends up being out of mind. That's why I want to encourage you to find a way to keep your vision, goals, and action steps in front of you. If you don't, your deadlines will come and go with your goals shoved deep into a desk drawer.

You know how you work best. For me, I keep my goals and action steps in an app on my laptop. For you, it might be a piece of paper you post on your refrigerator. No matter where you post them, you'll need to ensure that you set aside a specific time on your calendar to work on the action steps. If it's not calendared, it won't get done.

"In times of stress, I think a lot of us turn to nature. We know that it is calming and soothing to us. If you want to go deep, you look at a plant, look at what it goes through. It goes through darkness. It goes through renewal. It goes through growth. It goes through all of that. I think there's so much divine in nature that I think it reminds us about our own divine creation."[31]

MARY BROOKS, M.ED
Owner and creator of Sustainable Nutrition

Chapter 8
I WILL OVERCOME ANY CHALLENGE
"I will be strong and courageous in the face of any challenge."

Sound asleep in a low-budget motel outside Grand Canyon National Park, the ring of a cellphone wakes us both up.

"Hello?" answers Elijah in that confused, frantic way you pick up a call at 2am.

He hands the phone to me, and I hear heartbreaking news.

Two days prior, Elijah and I set out on a guys camping trip in Joshua Tree National Park, a couple of hours from Orange County, California. After shivering through a desert windstorm in a hand-me-down tent, I talked Elijah into extending our trip to the Grand Canyon, about 350 miles away. Since he was let go from his job on Friday, he had nowhere to be on Monday, and he needed something to distract him from the challenge of making a next career move.

"Hello?"

"Laura is in the hospital, and you need to be here."

While I was with the guys, Laura and our young daughter had taken a trip up to Santa Barbara to visit a friend who had recently given birth. The excitement of celebrating a new arrival turned to concern when my wife started to bleed.

At sixteen weeks pregnant, Laura rushed to a nearby hospital.
The baby had no heartbeat.

"Oh my God! Oh my God! Okay, um, we'll leave right away."

At 2am, we frantically grab our stuff and start the seven-hour drive back to Orange County to drop off Elijah and then a two-and-a-half-hour drive up to Santa Barbara by myself.

While I was enduring the longest drive of my life, Laura was giving birth to our second child. I could only imagine the emotional and physical pain she was enduring without me there.

I was confused and sad and anxious and didn't really know what to say.

By the time I arrived ten hours later, she was out of the hospital and resting at her friend's home. I wrapped my arms around her and hoped my embrace would embody the words that I didn't know how to articulate.

That was the first of three miscarriages we would experience. Each one was under unique circumstances, but one thing was the same. Laura was strong and courageous in the face of challenge and loss and grief. While I did my very best to be present and supportive, I knew that she was going through the experience at a different level than I was.

Your Challenges Shape You
In kindergarten, I broke my arm falling off the monkey bars. In fourth grade, I went flying across the pavement after a car hit me while I was riding my bike down an alley. In seventh grade, I wasn't chosen for the basketball team. When I was sixteen, I said goodbye to all my friends when my family moved from Kentucky to California. When I was a senior, my girlfriend broke up with me to go on a mission trip, and then the mission trip was canceled due to unrest in Yugoslavia.

In the years to come, I was fired from a job, couldn't land the ministry position I wanted, lost friendships, felt deeply confused about my direction in life, experienced extreme burnout, had an affair, filed for divorce, lost many relationships, and more. At this point, my guess is that you're comparing your challenges to my challenges.

"Oh my! I'm glad that didn't happen to me."
or
"Geez, he's had a pretty easy life!"

Here's what I know to be true...

1. There's no need to compare challenges with others.

Comparing our challenges does nothing to help anyone. There's no need to feel greater than or less than because of whatever you've experienced in life. Everyone has their own story, and everyone's story has deeply impacted how they see and operate in the world.

"You don't know what I've been through." If you feel like your challenges are so much greater than others, you're somehow degrading the pain that they've experienced. Their pain is their pain. When we feel the need to raise ourselves up, we're playing into a victim mentality to somehow increase our value based on what we've been through in life.

"I guess I've had a pretty easy life." Maybe you haven't gone through divorce or cancer or job loss, but you've experienced your own types of disappointment. Your pain is your pain. You can learn from any challenge if you're willing to, and you can become stronger and even more courageous in the process. Be thankful for your life, and know that you're not greater than or less than based on what you've experienced.

2. You can harness the power of previous challenges.

When you look back on the difficult things you've experienced in life, you have a life-changing choice. You can resent those experiences and focus on the pain, or you can choose to be thankful for what you learned in the process. You can be thankful for how you gained wisdom, how you grew stronger, and how you became more courageous.

Robin Sol Lieberman, creator of LIFEHONEY, shared with me, "The greatest gift of any of our breaks is the gift of personal growth, and part of that personal growth is compassion and empathy for others. When we have that, we change the world."[32]

I'm thankful that I was hit, broken up with, lost, burned out, and at rock bottom in a mental hospital. You know why? I'm a better person because of it. I see the world in a different way. I love my wife and kids at a deeper level. I am more present with people, and I have a greater level of compassion for people in need. More than anything, I am stronger and more courageous having gone through painful challenges.

I realize that you may have experienced abuse or brokenness at the hands of others, and that grieves me. In no way would I wish that on anyone. I'm not suggesting that you be thankful for the experience, but I'm inviting you to grieve the pain and embrace the strength and courage that is possible on this side.

3. We can be inspired by the strength and courage of others.
When we hear what others have gone through, we can celebrate their story and draw upon their strength and courage. Rather than saying, "I could never do that" or "I'm glad I'm not you", what if we said, "You've inspired me to live with strength and courage."...? When we take that posture, not comparing our challenges to theirs, we can celebrate their life and draw upon their strength and courage as we face challenges of our own. "If you can do it, I can do it!"

Women Who Inspire Me

I have the privilege of hosting conversations with numerous female leaders on the Inspiration Rising podcast, and I want to share just a few examples of women who inspire me. (You can listen to the full conversations online via the links in the endnotes.)

- At a young age, **Manna Kadar** came to the United States from Hong Kong with her mother and grandmother, and they lived in a rough Los Angeles neighborhood surrounded gang violence, drive-by shootings, and home invasion robberies. During high school, Manna worked and saved her money, which she used to purchase a cosmetics store that she grew to seven locations in six years before selling it. In 2012, Manna founded Manna Kadar Beauty as an international beauty brand, and her products are sold around the globe.[33]

- In 2014, **Sydney Williams** experienced tremendous loss in her life. Her friend committed suicide, her uncle died of brain cancer, another friend died from a base jump gone wrong, and her skydiving coach was convicted of raping a 14-year-old. Unexpectedly, she found herself on the receiving end of a Type 2 diabetes diagnosis, while grappling with unresolved trauma from a decades-old sexual assault. She retired as a competitive skydiver and hit the trail with her husband. Two long-distance hikes across Catalina Island helped Sydney understand a mind-body connection and healing power of nature, which she shares in her book entitled *Hiking My Feelings.*[34]

- **MacKenzie Koppa** started her marriage like most...with a desire for lifelong connection, love, and intimacy. Things took a turn when her husband became verbally, emotionally, and spiritually abusive. After fourteen years, she made the courageous decision to escape with her four children, who she had been homeschooling. During her drawn-out divorce, she has shared her story with courage and vulnerability in the hopes of helping other women caught in a cycle of abuse. MacKenzie now supports her family as a voiceover actor and podcaster.[35]

- **Maria Rabaino** had just started her second semester at college when she was in a horrible car crash with friends. The driver was killed, and Maria's back was broken at the L1 level, which left her paralyzed from the hips down. She spent a month and a half in the hospital learning how to adjust to her new life. Not only did she become independent faster than most people in her experience, but she found a new passion through dance by joining the Rollettes wheelchair dance team. She now speaks at schools about the dangers of getting in the car with someone who has been drinking, appeared in a commercial, was part of the first wheelchair dance team to ever perform at World of Dance, and competed at the ICU World Championships for the Para-cheer Hip Hop division.[36]

- **Jeanne Pepper Bernstein** is the mother of Blaze Bernstein, who was found dead on January 10, 2018, in Orange County, California. Eight days prior, the 19-year-old University of Pennsylvania sophomore had been reported missing while visiting his family on a break from college. One of Blaze's former high school classmates and a member of neo-Nazi terrorist group Atomwaffen Division was arrested and charged with murdering him. Because Blaze was both openly gay and Jewish, authorities declared that he was a victim of a hate crime. Jeanne and her husband, Gideon, formed Blaze It Forward, a movement that encourages people to honor Blaze's memory by spreading kindness.[37]

- **Michelle Dickinson** spent years playing the role of child caregiver to her mother who was diagnosed as bipolar, a mental illness that brings severe highs and lows. Because of her mom's depression, extreme mania, and sleepless nights, Michelle learned very quickly to read her mother's mood and know how her behavior should correspond. After years of therapy and healing, Michelle wrote *Breaking Into My Life: Growing Up with a Bipolar Parent and My Battle to Reclaim Myself* in an effort to raise awareness and compassion for those struggling with mental illness along with those who care for them, so that more people get the treatment and help they need and deserve.[38]

• **Kate Snowise** was in between work trips where she was presenting corporate resilience training when she felt some discomfort in one of her breasts. During the mammogram, the doctor noticed something unusual in the *other* breast. The next day, she had a biopsy, and on the following day, she was diagnosed with breast cancer just before her thirty-sixth birthday. Although she had no family history, Kate was told by her doctor that she most likely had cancer in both her breasts, which led her to choose to have a bilateral mastectomy. She continues to teach resilience in a corporate setting, coaches clients around the globe, and shares her story of hope with women.[39]

• At age 14, **Rhonda Britten** witnessed her father shoot and kill her mother and then take his own life...all on Fathers Day. Fearful of what others would think, she didn't share her story as she grew older. Eventually turning to alcohol to numb the trauma and three suicide attempts later, Rhonda realized that fear was at the root of her pain. In 2001, she started the Fearless Living Institute to help others overcome their fears. She is a bestselling author, speaker, and life coach who appeared on the reality TV series *Starting Over* from 2003-2006, where she won a Daytime Emmy.[40]

• After placing her newborn son for adoption, **Hope O. Baker** struggled with depression, addiction, and overcoming the stigma that surrounds birth mothers. In her book, *Finding Hope: A Birthmother's Journey Into the Light*, she shares her story of a successful, open adoption and all the heartache and light that came along the way. She is a passionate advocate for those on all sides of adoption. Hope visits her son regularly, and she currently lives with her loving partner and her wonderful step kids.[41]

- **Cameron Huddleston** started noticing signs that her mother, who was in her early 60's, was losing her memory. Even though Cameron was a financial journalist, she never thought to ask her mom questions about her finances or end of life wishes. She immediately sought help to create a power of attorney and health care power of attorney in order to avoid expensive, drawn out legal proceedings that Cameron had witnessed among friends. Although her mom no longer recognizes Cameron as her daughter, Cameron is empowered to ensure her mother is well cared for. As a result, Cameron wrote *Mom and Dad, We Need to Talk: How to Have Essential Conversations with Your Parents About Their Finances* to help others have these important conversations.[42]

Your name could be added to this list as well. If I were to include a paragraph about your story of overcoming challenges, what would it include? Perhaps you grew up in a tough family situation or you overcame a diagnosis or you made your way out of a bad relationship.

Here's what I know...*you've made it!* You are still alive, and you are stronger and more courageous because of what you've been through. You may not be where you want to be, but you're further along than you used to be.

Three Questions to Help You Overcome Challenges
As you're getting unstuck and taking your life to the next level, you will undoubtedly come up against challenges, and I want you to be prepared. I'm not sure when I started using that word...*challenge*...but it's a favorite. I don't generally use words like problem or trouble or difficulty. There's something about the word *challenge* that calls me to be more intentional and take action. Sure, you can call it an opportunity, but let's be honest. The stuff we're talking about is really hard to go through. It's really *challenging*.

Let's just say you had the opportunity to sit across the table from the inspiring women I just shared with you. In light of what they've experienced, I believe they would ask you three important questions.

1. **How are you cultivating a powerful, positive mindset?**
   No matter what challenge comes your way, your mind must be ready to deal with the situation. If you are prone to see the downside of life, if you look for the worst in other people, and if you speak words of negativity, you've probably been cultivating a negative mindset.

What would it look like to begin cultivating a positive perspective on life? For me, it's rooted in thankfulness. If I can find a way to be thankful for each experience, my mind (and heart) shifts toward powerful positivity.

When the grocery store line is long...I can be thankful that I have access to an unending amount of food.

When traffic is backed up on the freeway...I can be thankful I have a truck that runs great and gas in the tank.

When I have to pay taxes...I can be thankful that I generated income for my family.

When one of my family members is sick...I can be thankful for incredible modern technology and medical care.

As I'm finding something to be thankful for, my mind starts to see the positive in a situation. I'm not ignoring the pain of the moment, but I'm reframing it to see a *fresh* perspective.

Simultaneously, I can draw upon the memories of my past to propel me into the future.

If I can get through unending sports practices as a kid...
If I can get through painful physical injuries...
If I can get through moving across the country...
If I can get through intense education...
If I can get through losing a career...
If I can get through a broken marriage...
If I can get through losing friendships...
If I can get through burnout and breakdown...
I can get through my current challenge!

Another way I cultivate a powerful, positive mindset is through my words. How do you feel after saying...?

"I can't figure this out."
"I don't know what to do."
"I'll never be where I want to be."
"This is an absolute disaster."

I feel down just typing those words. Yuck! And yet, I say things like that from time to time. What if we started to say things like this instead...?

"I'll find a way."
"There's always a solution."
"I'm growing and learning every day."
"I can't wait to see how this turns out."

An ancient proverb says, "Words kill, words give life; they're either poison or fruit—you choose."[43]

Our words have intense power. When we bring words from our minds through our mouths, it's giving direction to our lives. By speaking words of negativity, we're cultivating a negative mindset...and ultimately a negative path. When we speak words of life and hope and courage, we're cultivating a powerful, positive mindset that is filling us up with courage and strength.

2. How are you cultivating resilience on a regular basis?

Resilience is your ability to recover quickly from the challenges you face. Anne Grady, best-selling author and TEDx speaker, shared with me, "Resilience is getting knocked down in pursuit of a goal or just life in general. It's your ability to get back up after you've been knocked down. It's your ability to not just survive challenging times and overcome adversity, but to thrive as a result and really grow from it."[44]

When Anne's son was born, he cried all day and all night. She and her husband went to multiple doctors, and nobody could tell them what was wrong. When their son was eighteen months old, her husband left, and Anne became a single mom. Things continued to escalate, and by the time he was three years old, her son tried to kill her with a pair of scissors. By the age of four, he was on his first anti-psychotic medication. At ages seven and ten, he was hospitalized. Soon after, a massage therapist noticed Anne had a swollen lymph node, which turned out to be a tumor the size of avocado in her salivary gland. It stretched her facial nerve so much that the right side of her face was completely paralyzed resulting in drooling, a speech impediment, and the inability to close her eye.

A couple of days after the initial surgery, a speck of dust scratched the cornea in the eye that wouldn't close, and her doctored wanted to put a gold weight into her upper eyelid and stitch the bottom eyelid. Before *that* surgery, she fell down the stairs and broke her foot in four places.

Anne shared, "I think the average person has five to six traumas in their lifetime, and I think I've had mine. I'm ready for the back half to be relaxing and easy."

No matter if your life resembles Anne's or not, you *will* face challenges and need resilience in order to bounce back from each experience. Envision yourself pouring resilience into a huge bucket each time you invest in a friendship, meditate, pray, exercise, read a soul-enriching book, eat healthy foods, experience nature, or intentionally reduce stress.

Anne emphasized, "Self-care is not selfish. It is a requirement for resilience. You cannot be resilient if you are not whole."

If you've filled up your resilience bucket over time, you'll be able to draw upon it when you're in need. If the bucket has run dry from a soul-withering lifestyle, it will be all that much harder to bounce back from a challenging experience. How are you filling up your resilience bucket regularly? (If it's not integrated into your daily life or intentionally calendared, it probably won't happen.)

3. How are you cultivating life-giving relationships?

In order to overcome challenges, not only do we need a positive mindset and a full bucket of resilience, but we also need life-giving relationships. If you've ever gone through a difficult season of life and experienced the support of close friends, you know how precious it is.

When I hit rock bottom, there were three friends and a therapist who walked with me through a dark night of the soul. They distracted me when I was an emotional mess. One of them slept at my apartment so I wouldn't be alone. They listened to my endless rambling through tears and encouraged me to get professional help. They re-decorated my apartment when I got out of the hospital, and they invited me to spend time with their families when my relationship with Laura and the kids was not good. On several occasions, one couple invited me to join them in the bedtime routine with their young kids as they prayed and tucked them in.

Absolutely priceless.

I will never forget those moments of sheer grace when *they* were investing in me when I desperately needed it.

Some people will be able to walk with you through the darkest moments of pain, and others won't. When others aren't available for you, it can be painful to not receive a call or check-in. The reality is...it's hard to care for people in pain. It takes a great deal of patience and grace to be with someone through the long road of divorce or cancer or addiction or homelessness.

It's one thing to call someone and share about your tough day at work. It's a whole other thing to have them walk with you for miles down Pacific Coast Highway as you cry your way back to your car, because it's the only place you know will feel safe. (Just brutal.)

While some people come out of the woodwork by sheer grace to help us in times of need, we're far better off cultivating life-giving relationships now rather than later. The truth is that we are wired for relationships, and we need other people all the time...not just in times of crisis.

While online friendships are wonderful, I believe there's nothing that can truly replace the joy of seeing someone face to face. The hug, the laughter, and eye-to-eye contact with another human being lets us know that we're not alone...something we need to know deep in our souls. You need to know that you're not alone in the journey of getting unstuck and clarifying what you really want in life...all while managing the kids and working a full-time job.

If you've moved away from high school or college friends...
If you've been feeling out of touch...
If you've felt distant from co-workers...
If you've never met your neighbors...
What would it look like to intentionally reach out and start cultivating life-giving relationships?

These types of friendships don't usually develop overnight. It requires an intentionality over time to cultivate a connection that goes beyond the surface.

Invite someone out to coffee. Ask a co-worker to join you for lunch. Have a couple over for dinner. Take your neighbor a plate of homemade cookies. Do whatever it takes to initially bridge the gap, and be genuinely interested in their lives. That's what we all want, right? When you're interested in them, they're more likely to be interested in you. It's worth the effort. It really is.

Bailey T. Hurley, writer and speaker with a passion for friendships, shared with me, "It's going to require us to say, 'I'm all in. I found someone that I've clicked with and connected with. We have some shared hobbies.' This makes me laugh a little bit, because it does sound like you're asking them to go steady with you. But to say to them, 'I've really enjoyed you, and I want to be friends. I want to take this to the next level. Can we make time every month that we can spend together? Can we put it on the calendar and make sure that this happens?'"[45]

I believe there's something inside of you...a vision...that you want to do or experience in the next six to twelve months. You know what it is. It's been echoing in your heart and mind for some time. This inspiration...this mental picture of your preferable future...is starting to become clear, and you're putting down goals and actions steps in writing.

Great job. You're doing it!

And yet, I don't want you to be surprised by challenges that arise. People may not support your dream like you had hoped. You may need to spend money that you had set aside for your dream on an unexpected medical bill or car repair. You may come down with a cold or flu right as you get started.

I hope and pray that none of those things actually happen, but if a challenge arises, I want you to know that you can get through it. Why? Because you're strong and courageous. It's part of your true identity, and you're already being intentional about cultivating resilience in your life. Keep going!

"The words 'out of control' imply that we're not the boss of us, right? It implies that we're not in charge of where our time is going, and there is some outside force that is in charge of it. I really think that it starts with a mindset shift back to, 'The only one in charge of where your time goes, moment by moment, is you.' There's an immediate shift back into agency when you realize, 'I literally have complete control over where I spend my time.' Now, you may have to tolerate some discomfort when other people don't like your choices about where you're spending your time, but ultimately, you have complete control. That's a very powerful force to harness."[46]

CHERYLANNE SKOLNICKI
Founder of The Brilliant Balance Company

"As a frazzled mom, you think the more you do...the better it is. When you're on that roller coaster, it's really hard to slow down. For me to tell somebody to take a pause and meditate, that may be way overwhelming. But, what I will say is...you do need to stop. The first thing to do is take a moment, look up, breathe, and tap in to your childlike manner. What's something that you haven't done in awhile that brings joy from within?"[47]

DR. BITA YADIDI
Doctor of Oriental Medicine

"Help one another. Share your experiences with each other. Help each other open up and transform each other's mindset. No matter what, where, or who you are, a man is not a financial plan. Alone we are strong, but together we are unstoppable."[48]

GENECIA ALLUORA
Former Miss Singapore
Founder of Soul Rich Woman

Chapter 9

I AM RISING UP - WILL YOU JOIN ME?

"My inspiration is rising"

When I allow my mind to wander back to some of the most inspirational moments of my life, it's interesting how sporting events, relationships, and spiritual experiences have made such an impact on me.

- Winning the Toy Bowl football championship as a young kid.
- Being chosen as a Little League all-star.
- Celebrating with my dad as the Western Kentucky University women's basketball team made it into the Final Four.
- Sensing a calling into full time ministry at a youth convention.
- Kissing Laura for the first time as we walked on the beach.
- Speaking to over 40,000 people in India.

Frankly, none of these inspiring moments compare to the birth of our two children...one naturally and one via C-section. The miracle of seeing a child enter the world (especially in light of the astronomical odds I shared in chapter one) is probably the most mind-blowing thing I've ever witnessed. I can't even imagine what it's like to carry a child for nine months and then give birth.

Women are to be revered for their strength and courage!

I'm also inspired on a daily basis by...
single parents who handle so many things by themselves,
dedicated teachers who go above and beyond for their students,
makers and artists who infuse beauty into our communities,
coaches who challenge us to go farther than we think we can go,
entrepreneurs who offer products and services that benefit our world,
and spiritual leaders who help us connect with the Divine.

There are so many people and experiences that can bring inspiration to our lives if we take the time to intentionally appreciate and marvel what is happening around us.

It's so easy to rush through our day in an effort to tackle our to-do list that we actually miss the inspiration of the moment. Rather than relegating inspiration to something we experience while watching a TED Talk or listening to a podcast, what if we started to anticipate inspiration in all the moments of life? You have the power to experience inspiration every day...

- **Stand in awe of the world around you.**
  Can you believe we live on a giant ball hurling through outer space? Isn't it incredible that water falls from the sky in order to sustain life? How can we not stand in awe of all the plants and animals we live among? From the unending sky above to the dirt below, you live in an awe-inspiring world, don't you? Be inspired.

- **Marvel at the beauty and strength of your body.**
  The next time you get out of the shower...take a look in the mirror. Can you believe the little baby who exited your mother's womb has grown and matured into the adult you're looking at now? Be thankful for the eyes that allow you to see, the nose that helps you smell, the ears that recognize sound. Look at your mouth. What an amazing tool it is to both speak and eat nourishing foods! Your body is an absolute miracle with all its intricacies.

- **Listen to inspiring stories, and tell your own!**
  We're all trying to make sense of this life, and the most common way we do this is through the telling of stories. We tell stories about how this world came into existence and what we're supposed be doing here. We tell stories about our past, present, and future. If you listen closely to a person's story (even your own), you can tell what role she's playing. Is she a victim, a martyr, a life-long learner, or an overcomer?

  We're inspired by stories of transformation and triumph. We love to hear about people who overcome the odds, come back from adversity, and choose to press on in the face of challenges. You are choosing to live that kind of life! You're not going to let anything stand in the way of embracing your true identity, uncovering your super powers, and bringing your inspiration...your vision...to the world. You are choosing to tell the story of your life through that lens of rising up. You're not a victim or a martyr. You're not going to lay down and allow the world to run over you. You are strong and courageous, and your story needs to be told.

I WILL RISE UP - WILL YOU JOIN ME?

I want you to know that *you* are in charge of your inspiration. When you wake up and feel uninspired, that is no one else's responsibility other than your own. If you pull the covers over your head and wait for inspiration to strike, you'll be waiting forever.

It's up to you and me to cultivate inspiration in our own lives. It may sound a bit silly to say, but that's why I love the last line of the Inspiration Rising Manifesto. It simply says, "My inspiration is rising."

My inspiration is *not* falling...it is *rising!*

My thoughts and words have the power to propel me into an upward cycle of inspiration or a downward tailspin of negativity. It's my choice where I direct my attention, and the results are always crystal clear.

When I focus on lack, hurdles, problems, gossip, and resentment, the clear result is a decline in my inspiration and motivation.

When I embrace my true identity...
When I look for opportunities to grow...
When I anticipate breakthroughs and blessings...
When I am thankful for what I already have...
When I celebrate the wins of others...
When I focus on my vision...
my inspiration rises!

The moments when I need to take these actions the most are when I'm feeling down. It's easy to be fired up about life and my next project when everything is going well and I'm filled with energy. It's hard when the car registration bill shows up, the sink is clogged, and I've gained a few extra pounds. In those moments, it's easier to allow those three small things to balloon into, "My life is horrible, and I should just go crawl into a hole."

Kate Crocco, author of *Thinking Like a Boss: Uncover and Overcome the Lies Holding You Back from Success*, shared, "I think we have a lot of fear, and we're afraid of what could happen if we move forward. Could I fail? Could I actually succeed? We tell ourselves that we need all these different things in order to move ahead, whether it's more time or feeling more ready or having more qualifications or having more people on board like our friends and family. It all starts in our minds. Just be willing to take that step to move ahead even when we're afraid."[49]

Frankly, one of the most effective ways for me to get out of a funk is dancing around and shouting "I am" statements (when no one is watching of course.) When I was in elementary school and learning multiplication tables, my dad would dance around the room saying, "12 x 12 is 144!" My dad is definitely not a dancer or prone to physical comedy, so his playfulness would lock the numbers into my mind and allow me to recall them with a smile during the test.

When I feel down and want to break out of the funk, I unleash my fancy dancing skills (inherited from my dad) and flail around as I shout, "I don't have to be or do anything else to be loved or enough. I am strong and courageous in the face of any challenge. My inspiration is rising!" The physical movement combined with powerful words starts to open up my mind and heart to new possibilities.

One Life to Live

With all that said, I have to tell you I'm concerned though. I'm concerned about all those women (and men) who are living an un-inspired life by simply trying to survive. Survival is the greatest enemy to living with inspiration. When you're merely surviving emotionally, relationally, physically, or financially, there's very little sense of awe or wonder or hope.

You have one life to live, and I want to help you live a rich, meaningful life. I know I've said it before, but your life is *so* important. No matter where you live or what you're experiencing right now…your life is valuable. If you're surrounded by dirty diapers and a sink full of dishes and just trying to make it through your day, your life is important. If you're trying to get that critical sales proposal done *and* get your kid to soccer practice on time, your life is important. If your kids have moved out and you're trying to uncover who you are in this new season, your life is important. Remember. You are inspired. You are enough. You are loved.

As you embrace your true identity each day, you will feel more and more confident to rise up and share your unique vision with the world. Don't let the thing that's important to you just fade into the distance. Don't allow it to die inside your heart. Whatever it is that you're longing to do or be or experience needs you to give it voice. We need to hear what's burning inside you. No matter how big or small it is in your mind…the world needs your vision to be unleashed.

John Wesley, an 18th century pastor and theologian, is often credited with saying, "Light yourself on fire with passion, and people will come from miles to watch you burn."[50] We're attracted to people who are on fire with passion. You know why? Because we long to feel the same thing.

When I hear someone talk with great passion about their love for cats or genetics or vintage typewriters, I get fired up. Why? Because *they're* fired up! When I feel someone else's passion, it fuels the passion within me. Will I become passionate about whatever they're interested in? Probably not, but that doesn't matter. I'm excited for them, and I am reminded about what's important to me.

As Jacqui Kennemer shared about her vision to become a flower farmer, I asked her what advice she has for you. "You have your own life, and you have your own dreams. What would life be like if you actually really did them? What if you were really happy? I think you just have to go for it. You don't know until you go. I think we pay so many prices in our life, because we feel like we have to do certain things. We feel like we have to show up a certain way, or we have to do these things so that we can maintain our bills, and blah, blah, blah. Life can look so many different ways if we just open up to it. Step into the opportunity. Embrace it with all your heart. Enjoy it, and have fun with it. Play with ideas and discover what it is that makes you come alive."[51]

How to Take Your Next Steps
Please don't put down this book without first making a plan to take clear action steps in your life. Yes, I want you to feel inspired, but more than anything, I want you to take action.

1. Write down your vision.
On the next page, I've given you space to capture a mental picture of your preferable future. This is your inspiration...your vision. It's the snapshot in time that embodies what you want to experience in the next six to twelve months. It could literally be anything!

This is *not* what your partner, kids, friends, or family want for your life. This is what *you* see and feel when you close your eyes and allow your mind to form a picture of what your heart desires.

What mental picture do you see coming to fruition in the next six to twelve months? When this vision is fulfilled in your life, what will you feel? *(Use the space below.)*

2. Set goals and action steps to bring the vision to fruition.

What goals do you need to reach in order to experience the mental picture you captured on the previous page? A goal is a tangible and measurable end result that can only be reached by executing a number of action steps. The goal is the result, and the action steps are the small, incremental steps that help you avoid overwhelm and empower you to take one step at a time. Your vision may require one or more goals depending on how big it is. Use the space below to capture goals, action steps, and accompanying deadlines.

Goal #1: _____

Deadline: _____

- Action Step: _____
  Deadline: _____

- Action Step: _____
  Deadline: _____

- Action Step: _____
  Deadline: _____

- Action Step: _____
  Deadline: _____

Goal #2: _____

Deadline: _____

- Action Step: _____
  Deadline: _____

- Action Step: _____
  Deadline: _____

- Action Step: _____
  Deadline: _____

- Action Step: _____
  Deadline: _____

3. Articulate the *why* behind your vision and goals.

There's a reason *why* you want to experience this vision. You may say, "It's just what I want." Okay, but why? There has to be a reason why this is so important to you. Articulating your *why* creates a deeper level of motivation to go after your goals.

Why do you want to experience this vision?

4. Determine what you will say *yes* and *no* to in your life.

In order to free up time to accomplish your new goals, you'll need to be honest with yourself about how you're spending your time and money. Currently, you're investing resources in activities, projects, and people that may or may not align with your goals.

For instance, you may be volunteering on multiple committees that all have a wonderful mission, but they may not align with your vision in this season of life. The amount of time invested may conflict with your need to be focused on your own goals. Saying no isn't a bad thing. In fact, it will empower you to rise.

Amy E. Smith, confidence coach and host of The Joy Junkie Show, shared with me, "You can say no with compassion, with grace, with kindness, with love, with concern, with empathy. I think it's a fallacy to even think that saying no equals meanness."[52]

What do you need to start saying *no* to in your life?

What do you need to start saying *yes* to?

Time to Rise Up

Now is the time. Not yesterday, not tomorrow, but *today*. You're not too late or too early. Now is the time to get started with the inspiration that's within your heart, but it *does* require you to rise up.

Rising up means that it's time to stop listening to those lies that you're not enough or it's too late or people won't understand. Rising up means that you're getting serious about embracing your true identity...the fact that you're inspired, enough, and loved.

Rising up means that you're not afraid to use your voice. Instead of cowering to those in power or those who have more experience, you're finding your voice by speaking up with your own thoughts, ideas, and opinions. Your voice is needed, so please speak up. We need to hear you!

Rising up means that you're not embarrassed by the dream in your heart. Rather than giving in to the expectations of others, you're courageously cultivating a vision that is meaningful to you personally. You're ready to share it with the world, because you know that the world needs what's inside of you.

Rising up means that you're willing to disappoint people you care about. It's not because you *want* to disappoint them, but you need to be true to what's important to you in this season of life. You're learning to articulate your vision and values without taking responsibility for the emotions or reactions of others.

Rising up means that you *are* taking responsibility for your own actions. You know that you have one life. You know there's something powerful inside of you. The Divine has breathed life into you and your vision, and now is the time.

I'm inviting you...even challenging you...to rise up with me!

Like never before, I believe our world needs women (and men) who are passionate about life. We've lived long enough under the anesthesia of complacency and mere survival. Now is your time to thrive.

Consider this your *reminder* that you are EMPOWERED TO RISE!

Please stop waiting around for someone to empower you to start that business, change your health, or go after the relationship you know you deserve.

You are *already* empowered!

The Divine has given you a precious life, and you are *already* inspired, enough, and loved. This is as much empowerment as you'll ever need.

Let's say it out loud one more time.

Inspiration Rising Manifesto

My life has been inspired from the moment of conception.
I am whole and complete just as I am.
I don't have to do or be anything else to be loved.

This is my true identity.

Embracing my inspired-ness, I am discovering my
unique way to bring inspiration to the world.
My life story, wiring, and strengths are my super powers,
and I am learning to use them with others
- for the sake of others.

I have access to all the resources I need to live out my inspiration,
and I will be strong and courageous in the face of any challenge.

My inspiration is rising.

I am rising up. Will you join me?

ACKNOWLEDGEMENTS

Thank you to **Laura** for your love, grace, and partnership.

Thank you to **Mom and Dad** for being faithful, for loving me and our family, and for believing in me.

Thank you to **Kristin Manna** for all your support in starting the podcast.

Thank you to **Kelsey Chapman** for inspiring me to write this book.

Thank you to **Stacey Robbins** for your constant support and encouragement throughout all the ups and downs of life. You are a true friend.

Thank you to **Jacqui Kennemer** for believing in me and cheering me on.

Thank you to **Rev. Sarah Heath** and **Rev. Molly Vetter** for giving me the opportunity to use my gifts and serve others.

Thank you to **Patricia Anderson** and **Catherine Paour** for your generous proofreading skills.

Thank you to the **Inspiration Rising Insiders** for helping choose the title, cover, and length of this book. You all inspire me!

Thank you to the **"Empowered to Rise" Book Launch Team** for believing in this project, reviewing the manuscript, and sharing this life-changing message with the world.

Beth Adkins, Patricia Anderson, Sebastiana Aprile, Raymond Arebalo, Leann Barna, Brittany Berk, Audrey Bill, Jessica Bishop, Brittany Breland, Janice Brodman, Elizabeth Brushwyler, Nina Callahan, Stephen Carroll, Janet Chismar, Lo-an Co, Shelley Coia, Rachel Copeland, Rebecca Craft, Liz Cruz, Patti Davidson, Shawn Davidson, Evan Davis, Kim DeAllen, Daniel Doty, Kevin Douglas, Steven Edmonds, Sara English, Lisa Faust, Sandy Fitzpatrick, Brenda Gard, Lisa Gonzalez, Susan Gorski, Christie Grimes, Kimberly Havlu, Katherine Hayes, Renee Henderson, Beth Hermitage, Carmen Higuchi, Gary Hinkle, Eleanor Hoppe, Cameron Huddleston, Dana Johnson, Misty Jones, Candace Joseph, Manna Kadar, Jacqui Kennemer, Lori Keyser-Boswell, James King, Jacqueline Lyon, Kristin Manna, Amber Mead, Rhonda Murray, Natalie Nelson, Marley Nelson-Rhoades, Barbie Nemeth, Ellen O'Callahan, Jennifer O'Neal, Catherine Paour, Pam Paradis, Rebecca Peper, Nathan Perez, Christopher Rayan, Laura Reed, J. Brooks Reid, Monica Rodriguez, Cindy Rogers, Tracy Rupp, Dawn Sharp, Sandra Shea, Jo Smith, Rick Solis, Pam Steiner, Aubrey Tester, Scott Thrailkill, Gina Tiritilli, Pamela Toole, Jennifer Truell, Sandy Tucker, Regina Vassia, Amy Verlennich, Tyler Walsh, Kristin Ward, James Wilson.

ENDNOTES

[1] Bex Bedford - www.InspoRising.com/BexBedford

[2] "Are You a Miracle? On the Probability of Your Being Born" Dr. Ali Binazir - www.huffpost.com/entry/probability-being-born_b_877853

[3] I recognize that we all have a different birth story. While many of us were deeply loved from the moment of our birth, some of us entered the world in the midst of a complicated scenario. If your biological parents weren't ready to care for you, I want you to know that the Divine was elated to have you enter this world. You were loved (and are loved) by the Divine and so many others.

[4] www.merriam-webster.com/words-at-play/the-origins-of-inspire

[5] Ali Tate Cutler - www.insporising.com/alitatecutler

[6] Sarah Small - www.InspoRising.com/SarahSmall

[7] Diane Kazer - www.InspoRising.com/DianeKazer

8 Chelsey Brooke - www.InspoRising.com/ChelseyBrooke

[9] Andrea Owen - www.InspoRising.com/AndreaOwen

[10] Karen Martel - www.InspoRising.com/KarenMartel

[11] Dr. Shannon Gulbranson - www.InspoRising.com/ShannonGulbranson

[12] Ephesians 1:4 - Bible Society New Zealand. (2018). NLT Bible: New Living Translation. Wellington, NZ.

[13] Lewis, C. S. (2017). The Four Loves. San Francisco: HarperOne.

[14] Carin Rockind - www.InspoRising.com/CarinRockind

[15] Jacqui Kennemer - www.InspoRising.com/JacquiKennemer

[16] Launch Your Life - www.InspoRising.com/Launch

[17] Michelle Coops - www.InspoRising.com/MichelleCoops

[18] Deming, W. E. (2018). Out of the Crisis. Cambridge: The MIT Press.

[19] Stacey Robbins - www.InspoRising.com/StaceyRobbins

[20] Kelsey Murphy - www.InspoRising.com/KelseyMurphy

[21] Lisa Cummings - www.InspoRising.com/LisaCummings

[22] https://www.myersbriggs.org/my-mbti-personality-type/mbti-basics/the-16-mbti-types.htm

[23] https://store.northpoint.org/products/one-not-everyone

[24] 1 Corinthians 12:26 - Bible Society New Zealand. (2018). NLT Bible: New Living Translation. Wellington, NZ.

[25] King, Martin Luther. "Letter from Birmingham Jail," April 16, 1963

[26] Julie Parker - www.InspoRising.com/JulieParker

[27] How the Launch Your Life Coaching Program Changed My Life - www.InspoRising.com/ChangeMyLife

[28] Vector Clinic Solutions - www.vectorclinicsolutions.com

[29] In Plain Sight: Stories of Hope and Freedom - www.inplainsightfilm.com

[30] Kelsey Chapman - www.InspoRising.com/KelseyChapman

[31] Mary Brooks - www.InspoRising.com/MaryBrooks

[32] Robin Sol Lieberman - www.InsporRising.com/RobinSolLieberman

[33] Manna Kadar - www.InspoRising.com/MannaKadar

[34] Sydney Williams - www.InspoRising.com/SydneyWilliams

[35] MacKenzie Koppa - www.InspoRising.com/MacKenzieKoppa

[36] Maria Rabaino - www.InspoRising.com/MariaRabaino

[37] Jeanne Bernstein - www.InspoRising.com/JeanneBernstein

[38] Michelle Dickinson - www.InspoRising.com/MichelleDickinson

[39] Kate Snowise - www.InspoRising.com/KateSnowise

[40] Rhonda Britten - www.InspoRising.com/RhondaBritten1

[41] Hope O. Baker - www.InspoRising.com/HopeOBaker

[42] Cameron Huddleston - www.InspoRising.com/CameronHuddleston

[43] Proverbs 18:21 - Peterson, E. H. (2004). The Message. Colorado Springs, CO: NavPress.

[44] Anne Grady - www.InspoRising.com/AnneGrady

[45] Bailey T. Hurley - www.InspoRising.com/BaileyHurley

[46] Cherylanne Skolnicki - www.InspoRising.com/CherylanneSkolnicki

[47] Dr. Bita Yadidi - www.InspoRising.com/DrBitaYadidiLive

[48] Genecia Alluora - www.InspoRising.com/GeneciaAlluora

[49] Kate Crocco - www.InspoRising.com/KateCrocco

[50] According to scholars, there is no evidence that John Wesley actually said this, but the principle is powerful nonetheless.

[51] Jacqui Kennemer - www.InspoRising.com/JacquiKennemer

[52] Amy E. Smith - www.InspoRising.com/AmyESmith

INSPIRATION
Rising

SUBSCRIBE TO THE PODCAST
www.InspoRising.com/Podcast

JOIN OUR PRIVATE FACEBOOK
COMMUNITY FOR SUPPORT
www.InspoRising.com/Insiders

FOLLOW US ON SOCIAL MEDIA
@InspoRising

LAUNCH YOUR LIFE COACHING
www.InspoRising.com/Launch